Storytime Crafts

Crazy Days

Kathryn Totten

Fort Atkinson, Wisconsin

Published by **UpstartBooks**

W5527 Highway 106

P.O. Box 800

Fort Atkinson, Wisconsin 53538-0800

1-800-448-4887

Acknowledgments

Thank you to my associates who suggested book titles and helped with testing the activities: Virginia Brace, Lisa Cole, Melissa Depper, Carolyn Pickett and Dee Requa.

Contents

Introduction

The purpose of this book is to make storytime planning easy. The themes are based on events in *Chase's Calendar of Events*. They have been chosen to appeal to children and to provide variety in storytimes. Each theme consists of an introduction activity, a suggested list of picture books and rest activities such as action rhymes, fingerplays and songs. Each theme includes a craft that is easy to complete. These storytime plans are most suitable for children ages two to six, but they can be adapted for infant storytimes or for story programs for children over age six.

Also included in this book are the words for selected traditional rhymes and songs. These rhymes and songs can be used frequently in storytimes as children enjoy participating in a familiar activity. Rhymes and songs are also excellent literacy tools. They improve memory, increase vocabulary and make acquiring language fun for children. Knowledge of a wide variety of traditional rhymes provides a good background in the culture and language of the child's community. The shared knowledge of traditional rhymes and songs also enhances the social experience for a child at storytime.

Participation stories add variety to storytimes. Storytelling enhances a read aloud program and should be included often. This book includes some original stories that have a repetitive element for the children to say along with the storyteller. Participation stories also include actions or gestures for the storyteller and the children. These stories serve as a model for adapting stories for participation. The participation stories in this book include suggestions for storytime themes when appropriate.

How to Use This Book

This book is divided into monthly themed programs. Each program begins with an introductory activity intended to interest and focus the attention of the children. Personalizing this introduction will help form a bond between you and your regular storytime attendees. Each program also contains an annotated book list and several rest activities. From these you may select those which appeal to you most, keeping in mind the audience for whom you are preparing. Personalize your storytime by adding your favorite rhymes, games and fingerplays and by including new picture books or old favorites that come to mind as you plan. For variety, you may try telling a story as part of your presentation.

Storytime Strategies

Experienced storytellers who work with young children use a number of simple strategies to improve the effectiveness of their programs. After introducing the theme, it is good practice to begin by reading the longest book on the program. Doing this while the children are fresh ensures that they will remain attentive for the entire book. Some storytellers invite the children to make comments after each book is read. This allows children to practice verbal skills and can help to build their vocabulary. It also helps to foster a feeling of unity in the audience. A rest activity helps to involve and refocus the children. Allowing the children to move their bodies in an organized way will reduce their tendency to move in a disorganized way. If the rest activities start with loud noises and large motions, then become quiet and still, this prepares the children for the next book. In a 30-minute storytime you may read up to three stories, depending upon their length and the general mood of the children on that particular day. It is always acceptable to delete something that was planned if necessary. The children may want a particular book repeated, and often they want to repeat the rest activities several times. The goals are to provide an exposure to literature, a warm social experience and a positive association with the storyteller and the library.

Age Appropriate Storytimes

The selection of books and rest activities for a storytime should match the development of the children who will attend. Here are some guidelines to assist storytime planners in the selection of materials.

Under 24 months

Infants and toddlers respond to books with large illustrations. The illustrations should be clear, simple and bright in color. Stories should be about familiar things: home, family, pets, toys, etc. Text should be very short. The storytime should include five or six bounce rhymes and fingerplays. A parent or caregiver always attends storytime with the child in this age group. Including traditional rhymes and songs for this age group has the added benefit of reinforcing the caregiver's knowledge of them. The ideal length for an infant storytime is 15 to 20 minutes.

Age 2

The two-year-old child enjoys the familiarity of a standard opening and closing activity for storytime. Participation in the action rhymes may be inconsistent. Books with rhyming text and repetitive elements are appropriate. Text should be short. A two-year-old child will have the best attention span at the beginning of the storytime. This is the time to try reading a book with longer text. Stories should be about familiar things: family, going to the park or zoo, baby animals, bedtime, etc. A short craft that requires the use of a glue stick or jumbo size crayons can be attempted. A parent or caregiver usually attends storytime with the child and can assist with the craft. The ideal length for a two-year-old storytime is 20 to 25 minutes.

Age 3

At age three children are becoming verbal. Participation in action rhymes and songs will be much better. The three-year-old child will enjoy participation stories. Books with repetitive elements can be especially fun when the children are coaxed to say the recurring phrase with the reader. Stories can include a wider variety of themes: helping, siblings, holidays, humor. Books with longer text can be introduced. Three-year-old children enjoy hearing a book that is familiar to them, so books that they heard at two-year-old storytime will be appropriate. A short craft can be completed independently. The ideal length for a three-year-old storytime is 30 minutes.

Ages 4-6

Preschool age children enjoy showing off their knowledge. They will enjoy participating with counting books, alphabet books and books with sounds. They may interrupt the reading with comments, but can be persuaded to wait and talk between the stories. Stories with longer text, more humorous situations and more tension can be included. Folktales are ideal for this age group. Crafts will be completed with greater individuality. The ideal length for preschool storytime is 30 minutes.

Family Storytime

Storytimes for mixed ages must include a variety of activities. Rest activities interspersed with books of varying lengths will help ensure that toddlers and older children enjoy the storytime. Music appeals to people of all ages. A cappella singing, recorded music and rhythm instruments should be used frequently. The addition of a guitar, ukulele or Autoharp will enhance the experience. The use of visual aids improves attention span for longer stories. Puppets, flannel board figures and real items such as costumes, hats or live animals make the family storytime memorable.

Songs to Sing

"A Tisket, A Tasket"

A tisket, a tasket,
A green and yellow basket.
I wrote a letter to my love
And on the way I lost it.

I lost it, I lost it,
On the way I lost it.
A little girl picked it up
And put it in her pocket.

"Animal Fair"

I went to the animal fair,
The birds and the beasts were there,
The big baboon by the light of the moon,
Was combing his auburn hair.

The monkey smelled a skunk,
And fell on the elephant's trunk.
The elephant sneezed,
And fell on his knees,
And he's lucky he missed the monk.

"Ants Go Marching"

The ants go marching one by one.
Hurrah! Hurrah!
The ants go marching one by one.
Hurrah! Hurrah!
The ants go marching one by one;
The little one stops to suck his thumb,
And they all go marching,
Down into the ground,
To get out of the rain.
Boom, boom, boom!

The ants go marching two by two.
Hurrah! Hurrah!
The ants go marching two by two.
Hurrah! Hurrah!
The ants go marching two by two;
The little one stops to tie his shoe,
And they all go marching,
Down into the ground,
To get out of the rain.
Boom, boom, boom!

Next verses:

The ants go marching three by three;
The little one stops to ride a bee.

The ants go marching four by four;
The little one stops to ask for more.

The ants go marching five by five;
The little one stops to jump and dive.

The ants go marching six by six;
The little one stops to pick up sticks.

The ants go marching seven by seven;
The little one stops to write with a pen.

The ants go marching eight by eight;
The little one stops to roller skate.

The ants go marching nine by nine;
The little one stops to drink and dine.

The ants go marching ten by ten;
The little one stops to shout,
"THE END!!"

"Baby Bumblebee"

I'm bringing home my baby bumblebee,
Won't my mommy be so proud of me.
I'm bringing home my baby bumblebee.
Ooh, it stung me!

I'm squishing up my baby bumblebee,
Won't my mommy be so proud of me.
I'm squishing up my baby bumblebee.
Ooh, it's all over me!

"Bingo"

There was a farmer had a dog,
And Bingo was his name-o.
B-I-N-G-O!
B-I-N-G-O!
B-I-N-G-O!
And Bingo was his name-o!

There was a farmer had a dog,
And Bingo was his name-o.
(clap)-i-n-g-o!
(clap)-i-n-g-o!
(clap)-i-n-g-o!
And Bingo was his name-o!

(Continue replacing letters one at a time with a clap.)

"Boom, Boom! Ain't It Great to Be Crazy?"

A horse and a flea and three blind mice,
Sat on a curbstone shooting dice.
The horse he slipped and fell on the flea.
"Whoops!" said the flea, "There's a horse on me!"

Chorus:

Boom, boom! Ain't it great to be crazy?
Boom, boom! Ain't it great to be crazy?
Silly and foolish the whole day long.
Boom, boom! Ain't it great to be crazy?

Way down south where bananas grow,
A flea stepped on an elephant's toe.
The elephant cried, with tears in his eyes,
"Why don't you pick on someone your own size?"

Repeat Chorus

Way up north where there's ice and snow,
There lived a penguin and his name was Joe.
He got so tired of black and white,
He wore pink slacks to the dance last night!

Repeat Chorus

"Do Your Ears Hang Low?"

Do your ears hang low?
Do they wobble to and fro?
Can you tie them in a knot?
Can you tie them in a bow?
Can you throw them over your shoulder,
Like a continental soldier?
Do your ears hang low?

"Donut Song"

Well, I walked around the corner,
And I walked around the block,
And I walked right into the donut shop.

And I picked up a donut,
Right fresh from the grease,
And I handed the lady a five-cent piece.

Well, she looked at the nickel,
And she looked at me.
And she said, "This nickel is no good you see."

"There's a hole in the middle
And it goes right through."
And I said, "There's a hole in my donut, too."

"Down by the Station"

Down by the station,
Early in the morning,
See the little pufferbellies,
All in a row.

See the station master,
Turn the little handle,
Puff, puff, toot, toot,
Off we go!

"The Farmer in the Dell"

The farmer in the dell,
The farmer in the dell.
Hi-ho the dairy-o,
The farmer in the dell.

The farmer takes a wife,
The farmer takes a wife.
Hi-ho the dairy-o,
The farmer takes a wife.

Repeat with:

The wife takes a child.

The child takes a dog.

The dog takes a cat.

The cat takes a rat.

The rat takes the cheese.

The cheese stands alone.

"Head, Shoulders, Knees and Toes"

Head, shoulders, knees and toes,
Knees and toes.
Head, shoulders, knees and toes,
Knees and toes.
Eyes, and ears, and mouth, and nose.
Head, shoulders, knees and toes,
Knees and toes.

"Here We Go 'Round"

Here we go 'round the mulberry bush,
The mulberry bush,
The mulberry bush.
Here we go 'round the mulberry bush,
So early in the morning.

This is the way we wash our clothes,
Wash our clothes,
Wash our clothes.
This is the way we wash our clothes,
So early Monday morning.

This is the way we iron our clothes,
Iron our clothes,
Iron our clothes.
This is the way we iron our clothes,
So early Tuesday morning.

This is the way we scrub the floor,
Scrub the floor,
Scrub the floor.
This is the way we scrub the floor,
So early Wednesday morning.

This is the way we mend our clothes,
Mend our clothes,
Mend our clothes.
This is the way we mend our clothes,
So early Thursday morning.

This is the way we sweep the floor,
Sweep the floor,
Sweep the floor.
This is the way we sweep the floor,
So early Friday morning.

This is the way we bake our bread,
Bake our bread,
Bake our bread.
This is the way we bake our bread,
So early Saturday morning.

This is the way we get dressed up,
Get dressed up,
Get dressed up.
This is the way we get dressed up,
So early Sunday morning.

Here we go 'round the mulberry bush,
The mulberry bush,
The mulberry bush.
Here we go 'round the mulberry bush,
So early in the morning.

"Hush, Little Baby"

Hush, little baby, don't say a word.
Papa's going to buy you a mockingbird.
If the mockingbird won't sing,
Papa's going to buy you a diamond ring.
If the diamond ring turns to brass,
Papa's going to buy you a looking glass.
If the looking glass gets broke,
Papa's going to buy you a billy goat.
If the billy goat runs away,
Papa's going to buy you another today.

"If You're Happy"

If you're happy and you know it,
Clap your hands.

If you're happy and you know it,
Clap your hands.

If you're happy and you know it
And you really want to show it,
If you're happy and you know it,
Clap your hands.

If you're happy and you know it,
Stamp your feet.

If you're happy and you know it,
Stamp your feet.

If you're happy and you know it
And you really want to show it,
If you're happy and you know it,
Stamp your feet.

If you're happy and you know it,
Shout, "We are!"

If you're happy and you know it,
Shout, "We are!"

If you're happy and you know it
And you really want to show it,
If you're happy and you know it,
Shout, "We are!"

If you're happy and you know it,
Clap your hands, stamp your feet, shout, "We are!"

If you're happy and you know it,
Clap your hands, stamp your feet, shout, "We are!"

If you're happy and you know it
And you really want to show it,
If you're happy and you know it,
Clap your hands, stamp your feet, shout, "We are!"

"I've Been Working On the Railroad"

I've been working on the railroad,
All the live-long day.
I've been working on the railroad,
Just to pass the time away.

Don't you hear the whistle blowing?
Rise up so early in the morn'.
Don't you hear the captain shouting,
Dinah blow your horn!

Someone's in the kitchen with Dinah,
Someone's in the kitchen I know-oh-oh-oh.
Someone's in the kitchen with Dinah,
Strumming on the old banjo.

And singing Fee Fi Fid-dle-ee aye oh!
Fee Fi Fid-dle-ee aye oh oh oh oh!
Fee Fi Fid-dle-ee aye oh!
Strumming on the old ban-jo!

"Itsy Bitsy Spider"

The itsy bitsy spider,
Climbed up the water spout.
Down came the rain
And washed the spider out.
Out came the sun
And dried up all the rain.
And the itsy bitsy spider,
Climbed up the spout again.

"London Bridge"

London Bridge is falling down,
Falling down, falling down.
London Bridge is falling down,
My fair lady.

Take a key and lock her up,
Lock her up, lock her up.
Take a key and lock her up,
My fair lady.

"Mary Had a Little Lamb"

Mary had a little lamb,
Little lamb, little lamb.
Mary had a little lamb,
Its fleece was white as snow.

Everywhere that Mary went,
Mary went, Mary went.
Everywhere that Mary went,
The lamb was sure to go.

It followed her to school one day,
School one day, school one day.
It followed her to school one day,
Which was against the rules.

It made the children laugh and play,
Laugh and play, laugh and play.
It made the children laugh and play,
To see a lamb at school.

"Muffin Man"

Oh, do you know the muffin man,
The muffin man, the muffin man?
Oh, do you know the muffin man,
Who lives on Drury Lane?

Oh yes, I know the muffin man,
The muffin man, the muffin man.
Oh yes, I know the muffin man,
Who lives on Drury Lane.

Now we all know the muffin man,
The muffin man, the muffin man.
Now we all know the muffin man,
Who lives on Drury Lane.

"Over the River and Through the Woods"

Over the river and through the woods,
To grandmother's house we go.
The horse knows the way,
To carry the sleigh,
Through the white and drift-ed snow-oh.

Over the river and through the woods,
Oh how the wind does blow!
It stings the toes, and bites the nose,
As o-ver the ground we go.

Over the river and through the woods,
To have a first-rate play.
Oh hear the bells ring,
"Ting-a-ling-ling!"
Hurrah for Thanksgiving Day.

Over the river and through the woods,
Trot fast my dapple gray!
Spring over the ground,
Like a hunting hound!
For this is Thanksgiving Day.

Over the river and through the woods,
And straight through the barnyard gate.
We seem to go extremely slow.
It is so hard to wait!

Over the river and through the woods,
Now grandmother's cap I spy!
Hurrah for the fun!
Is the pudding done?
Hurrah for the pumpkin pie!

Over the river and through the woods,
To grandmother's house we go.
The horse knows the way,
To carry the sleigh,
Through the white and drifted snow-oh.

Over the river and through the woods,
Oh how the wind does blow!
It stings the toes, and bites the nose,
As over the ground we go.

"Pop Goes the Weasel"

All around the mulberry bush,
The monkey chased the weasel.
The monkey thought 'twas all in fun.
Pop! goes the weasel.

A penny for a spool of thread,
A penny for a needle.
That's the way the money goes.
Pop! goes the weasel.

"Rock-a-bye Baby"

Rock-a-bye, baby, on the treetop;
When the wind blows the cradle will rock.
When the bough breaks, the cradle will fall,
And down will come baby, cradle and all.

"Row, Row, Row Your Boat"

Row, row, row your boat,
Gently down the stream.
Merrily, merrily, merrily, merrily,
Life is but a dream.

"Sailing, Sailing"

Sailing, sailing, over the bounding main.
For many a stormy wind shall blow,
E'er Jack comes home again.
Oh, sailing, sailing, over the bounding main.
For many a stormy wind shall blow,
E'er Jack comes home again.

"Twinkle, Twinkle, Little Star"

Twinkle, twinkle, little star,
How I wonder what you are.
Up above the world so high,
Like a diamond in the sky.
Twinkle, twinkle, little star,
How I wonder what you are.

"Where is Thumbkin?"

Where is Thumbkin?
Where is Thumbkin?
Here I am, here I am.
How are you today?
Very well, thank you.
Go away, go away.

Where is Pointer?
Where is Pointer?
Here I am, here I am.
How are you today?
Very well, thank you.
Go away, go away.

Where is Ring Man?
Where is Ring Man?
Here I am, here I am.
How are you today?
Very well, thank you.
Go away, go away.

Where is Small Man?
Where is Small Man?
Here I am, here I am.
How are you today?
Very well, thank you.
Go away, go away.

"Where, Oh, Where Has My Little Dog Gone?"

Where, oh, where has my little dog gone?
Oh, where, oh, where can he be?
With his tail cut short and his hair cut long,
Oh, where, oh, where can he be?

"You Are My Sunshine"

You are my sunshine, my only sunshine.
You make me happy when skies are gray.
You'll never know dear, how much I love you.
So please don't take my sunshine away.

Nursery Rhymes to Share

A, B, C

A, B, C, tumble down D.
The cat's in the cupboard
And can't see me.

A Diller, a Dollar

A diller, a dollar,
A ten o'clock scholar.
What makes you come so soon?
You used to come at ten o'clock,
But now you come at noon.

An Apple a Day

An apple a day,
Sends the doctor away.
Apple in the morning,
Doctor's warning.
Roast apple at night,
Starves the doctor outright.
Eat an apple going to bed,
Knock the doctor on the head.
Three each day, seven days a week,
Ruddy apple, ruddy cheek.

Baa, Baa, Black Sheep

Baa, baa, black sheep,
Have you any wool?
Yes, sir, yes, sir,
Three bags full;
One for the master,
And one for the dame,
And one for the little boy,
Who lives down the lane.

Baby Bunting

Bye, Baby Bunting,
Daddy's gone a-hunting,
To get a little rabbit skin,
To wrap my Baby Bunting in.

Birds of a Feather

Birds of a feather flock together,
And so will pigs and swine.
Rats and mice will have their choice,
And so will I have mine.

Bobby Shaftoe

Bobby Shaftoe went to sea,
Silver buckles on his knee.
He'll come back and marry me,
Pretty Bobby Shaftoe.

Bobby Shaftoe's fine and fair,
Combing down his auburn hair.
He's my friend for evermore,
Pretty Bobby Shaftoe.

Burnie Bee

Burnie Bee, Burnie Bee,
Tell me when your wedding be.
If it be tomorrow day,
Take your wings and fly away.

Cat Came Fiddling

A cat came fiddling out of a barn,
With a pair of bagpipes under her arm.
She could sing nothing but fiddle dee dee,
The mouse has married the bumblebee.
Pipe, cat; dance, mouse;
We'll have a wedding at our good house.

Come to the Window

Come to the window,
My baby, with me,
And look at the stars,
That shine on the sea!

There are two little stars,
That play bo-peep,
With two little fish,
Far down in the deep.

And two little frogs,
Cry, "Neap, neap, neap."
I see a dear baby,
That should be asleep.

Diddle Diddle Dumpling

Diddle, diddle, dumpling,
My son, John,
Went to bed,
With his trousers on.
One shoe off,
And one shoe on!
Diddle, diddle, dumpling,
My son, John!

Face Play

Knock at the door. *(Forehead tap.)*
Ring the bell. *(Tug each ear.)*
Lift the latch. *(Eyelids raise.)*
Walk in. *(Open mouth and pop finger inside.)*
Take a chair. *(Touch right cheek.)*
Sit down. *(Touch left cheek.)*
Good morning, sir! *(Finger on chin.)*

Fish Story

One, two, three, four, five—
Once I caught a fish alive.
Six, seven, eight, nine, ten—
Then I let it go again.
Why did I let it go?
Because it bit my finger so.
Which finger did it bite?
The little finger on the right.

Five Little Pigs

This little pig went to market.
This little pig stayed home.
This little pig had roast beef.
This little pig had none.
This little pig cried, "Wee, wee, wee, wee!"
All the way home.

Hark! Hark!

Hark! Hark! The dogs do bark,
The beggars are coming to town.
Some in rags,
And some in tags,
And one in a velvet gown!

Here Am I

Here am I, little Jumping Joan;
When nobody's with me,
I'm always alone.

Here is the Church

Here is the church, and here is the steeple;
Open the door and here are the people.
They stand up to sing,
They kneel down to pray.
And when the bell rings they all run away.

Hey, Diddle Diddle

Hey, diddle diddle,
The cat and the fiddle,
The cow jumped over the moon.
The little dog laughed,
To see such sport,
And the dish ran away with the spoon.

Hickory Dickory Dock

Hickory, dickory, dock,
The mouse ran up the clock.
The clock struck one,
The mouse ran down!
Hickory, dickory, dock.

Higglety Pigglety

Higglety, pigglety, my black hen,
She lays eggs for gentlemen.
Gentlemen come every day,
To see what my black hen doth lay.
Sometimes nine, and sometimes ten.
Higglety, pigglety, my black hen.

Hot Cross Buns

Hot cross buns!
Hot cross buns!
One a penny, two a penny,
Hot cross buns!
Hot cross buns!
Hot cross buns!
If you have no daughters,
Give them to your sons!

Humpty Dumpty

Humpty Dumpty sat on a wall.
Humpty Dumpty had a great fall.
All the king's horses and all the king's men,
Couldn't put Humpty together again!

I Had a Little Nut Tree

I had a little nut tree, nothing would it bear,
But a silver nutmeg and a golden pear.
The King of Spain's daughter came to visit me,
And all for the sake of my little nut tree.
I skipped over water, I danced over sea,
And all the birds in the air couldn't catch me.

I See the Moon

I see the moon,
And the moon sees me;
God bless the moon,
And God bless me!

Ice Cream, a Penny, a Lump

Ice cream, a penny, a lump!
The more you eat, the more you jump.

It's Raining

It's raining, it's pouring;
The old man is snoring.
Bumped his head
And he went to bed
And he couldn't get up in the morning.

Jack and Jill

Jack and Jill
Went up the hill
To fetch a pail of water.
Jack fell down
And broke his crown,
And Jill came tumbling after.

Ladybug, Ladybug

Ladybug! Ladybug!
Fly away home.
Your house is on fire
And your children all gone.

Little Bo Peep

Little Bo Peep has lost her sheep
And can't tell where to find them.
Leave them alone, and they'll come home,
Wagging their tails behind them.

Little Boy Blue

Little Boy Blue, come blow your horn,
The sheep's in the meadow, the cow's in the corn.
Where is the boy who looks after the sheep?
He's under a haycock, fast asleep.
Will you wake him? No, not I,
For if I do, he's sure to cry.

Little Jack Horner

Little Jack Horner
Sat in a corner,
Eating a Christmas pie.
He stuck out his thumb
And pulled out a plum,
And said, "What a good boy am I!"

Little Miss Muffet

Little Miss Muffet, sat on a tuffet,
Eating her curds and whey;
Along came a spider,
Who sat down beside her
And frightened Miss Muffet away.

Old Mother Hubbard

Old Mother Hubbard,
Went to the cupboard,
To fetch her poor dog a bone.
But when she came there,
The cupboard was bare,
And so the poor dog had none.

One for the Money

One for the money,
Two for the show,
Three to make ready,
And four to go!

One, Two, Buckle My Shoe

One, two, buckle my shoe;
Three, four, knock at the door;
Five, six, pick up sticks;
Seven, eight, lay them straight;
Nine, ten, a good fat hen;
Eleven, twelve, dig and delve;
Thirteen, fourteen, maids a-courting;
Fifteen, sixteen, maids a-kissing;
Seventeen, eighteen, maids a-waiting;
Nineteen, twenty, I've had plenty.

Pat-A-Cake

Pat-a-cake, pat-a-cake, baker's man,
Bake me a cake as fast as you can.
Roll it, and prick it, and mark it with a "B"
And put it in the oven for baby and me!

Pease Porridge Hot

Pease porridge hot,
Pease porridge cold,
Pease porridge in the pot
Nine days old.
Some like it hot,
Some like it cold,
Some like it in the pot
Nine days old.

Peter Peter Pumpkin Eater

Peter, Peter, pumpkin eater,
Had a wife and couldn't keep her.
He put her in a pumpkin shell
And there he kept her very well.

Polly, Put the Kettle On

Polly, put the kettle on,
Polly, put the kettle on,
Polly, put the kettle on,
We'll all have tea.

Sukey, take it off again,
Sukey, take it off again,
Sukey, take it off again,
They've all gone away.

Rain, Rain, Go Away

Rain, rain, go away;
Come again another day;
Little Johnny wants to play.

Red Sky At Night

Red sky at night,
Shepherd's delight;
Red sky in the morning,
Shepherd's warning.

Ring Around the Rosies

Ring around the rosies,
A pocket full of posies,
Ashes! Ashes!
We all fall down!

Rub-a-Dub-Dub

Rub-a-dub-dub,
Three men in a tub.
And who do you think they be?
The butcher, the baker, the candlestick-maker
All scrubbing their way out to sea.

Sally Go Round the Sun

Sally go round the sun,
Sally go round the moon,
Sally go round the chimney pots,
On a Saturday afternoon.

Sing a Song of Sixpence

Sing a song of sixpence,
A pocket full of rye;
Four and twenty blackbirds,
Baked in a pie.
When the pie was opened,
They all began to sing.
Now, wasn't that a dainty dish,
To set before the King?

The King was in his counting house,
Counting out his money;
The Queen was in the parlor,
Eating bread and honey.
The maid was in the garden,
Hanging out the clothes.
Along there came a big blackbird,
And snipped off her nose!

Sleep, Baby, Sleep

Sleep, baby, sleep.
Thy papa guards the sheep,
Thy mama shakes the dreamland tree,
And from it fall sweet dreams for thee.
Sleep, baby, sleep.

Sleep, baby, sleep.
Our cottage vale is deep,
The little lamb is on the green,
With woolly fleece so soft and clean.
Sleep, baby, sleep.

Sleep, baby, sleep.
Down where the woodbines creep,
Be always like the lamb so mild,
A kind and sweet and gentle child.
Sleep, baby, sleep.

Star Light, Star Bright

Star light, star bright,
First star I see tonight.
I wish I may, I wish I might,
Have the wish I wish tonight.

Teddy Bear, Teddy Bear

Teddy bear, teddy bear,
Turn around.
Teddy bear, teddy bear,
Touch the ground.

Teddy bear, teddy bear,
Show your shoe.
Teddy bear, teddy bear,
That will do.

Teddy bear, teddy bear,
Go upstairs.
Teddy bear, teddy bear,
Say your prayers.

Teddy bear, teddy bear,
Turn out the light.
Teddy bear, teddy bear,
Say good night.

There Was a Little Turtle

There was a little turtle,
Who lived in a box.
He swam in the puddles,
And climbed on the rocks.

He snapped at the mosquito,
He snapped at the flea.
He snapped at the minnow,
And he snapped at me.

He caught the mosquito,
He caught the flea.
He caught the minnow,
But he didn't catch me!

There Was an Old Woman

There was an old woman tossed up in a blanket,
Seventeen times as high as the moon.
But where she was going, no mortal could tell it,
For under her arm, she carried a broom.

"Old woman, old woman, old woman," quoth I,
"Whither, ah whither, ah whither so high?"
"To sweep the cobwebs from the sky."
"May I come with you?"
"Aye, by and by."

This Little Froggy

This little froggy took a big leap.
This little froggy took a small.
This little froggy leaped sideways.
And this little froggy not at all.
And this little froggy went,
Hippity, hippity, hippity hop, all the way home.

Three Blind Mice

Three blind mice,
See how they run!
They all ran after a farmer's wife,
Who cut off their tails with a carving knife.
Did you ever see such a sight in your life,
As three blind mice?

Three Little Kittens

Three little kittens,
They lost their mittens,
And they began to cry,
Oh, mother, dear,
We sadly fear,
Our mittens we have lost.
What! Lost your mittens,
You naughty kittens,
Then you shall have no pie.
Meow, meow,
Then you shall have no pie.

The three little kittens,
They found their mittens,
And they began to cry,
Oh, mother, dear,
See here, see here,
Our mittens we have found.

What, found your mittens,
Then you're good kittens,
And you shall have some pie.
Purr-rr, purr-rr,
Then you shall have some pie.

Three little kittens,
Put on their mittens,
And soon ate up the pie.
Oh, mother, dear,
We sadly fear,
Our mittens we have soiled.
What! Soiled your mittens,
You naughty kittens,
And they began to sigh.
Meow, meow,
And they began to sigh.

The three little kittens,
They washed their mittens,
And hung them out to dry.
Oh, mother, dear,
Do you not hear,
Our mittens we have washed?
What! Washed your mittens?
Then you're good kittens!
But I smell a rat close by.
Meow, meow,
We smell a rat close by.

To Market

To market, to market, to buy a fat pig,
Home again, home again, jiggety jig.
To market, to market, to buy a fat hog,
Home again, home again, jiggety jog.

Wee Willie Winkie

Wee Willie Winkie,
Runs through the town,
Upstairs and downstairs,
In his nightgown.
Rapping at the windows,
Crying through the lock,
"Are the children all in bed?
For it's now eight o'clock."

Wise Old Owl

A wise old owl sat in an oak,
The more he heard, the less he spoke;
The less he spoke, the more he heard;
Why aren't we all like that wise old bird?

Participation Stories to Tell

Three Robins in the Nest

Once there were three very hungry baby robins in a nest. They looked up and down and all around for something good to eat.

The first little robin said, "I've got to get me a wiggly worm!" He shook one wing. He shook the other. Then the first little robin flew off in a flutter.

Now there were two baby robins in a nest. They were very hungry. The robins looked up and down and all around for something good to eat.

The second little robin said, "I've got to get me a wiggly worm!" He shook one wing. He shook the other. Then the second little robin flew off in a flutter.

Now there was one baby robin in a nest. He was very hungry. The robin looked up and down and all around for something good to eat.

The third little robin said, "I've got to get me a wiggly worm!" He shook one wing. He shook the other. But he did not fly off in a flutter. He peeked over the edge of the nest at the ground below. It seemed like such a long, long way down.

A shadow passed over the little robin in the nest. It was the shadow of a fluffy cloud floating by. The third little robin said, "I've got to get me a wiggly worm! Fluffy Cloud, how about a ride?"

"Sorry, friend," said the fluffy cloud. "I cannot carry you, but your wings can."

Now there was still one baby robin in a nest. He was very hungry. The robin looked up and down and all around for something good to eat.

The third little robin said, "I've got to get me a wiggly worm!" He shook one wing. He shook the other. But he did not fly off in a flutter. The ground still seemed like such a long, long way down.

A honeybee buzzed by the little robin in the nest. He was gathering pollen from the apple tree blossoms. The third little robin said, "I've got to get me a wiggly worm! Honeybee, how about a ride?"

"Sorry, friend," said the honeybee. "I cannot carry you, but your wings can."

There was still one baby robin in a nest. He was more than very hungry. He was famished! He shook one wing. He shook the other. He looked at the ground far below. "It is too far," he said. So the little robin closed one eye. He shook one wing. He shook the other. He looked at the ground far below. "It is still too far," he said. So the little robin closed the other eye. He shook one wing. He shook the other. All at once he flew off in a flutter. His wings carried him down, down, down ever so gently to the ground below. When he opened his eyes, guess what he saw? He saw a beautiful, juicy, wiggly worm! Just like that, he ate it.

Notes on Telling the Story

Before telling the story, teach the children to say the phrase,

"I've got to get me a wiggly worm." Use a funny voice, to imitate a squeaky little bird. Develop a signal so the children will know when to say the phrase. You might make your hand "talk," or rub your tummy, for example.

Related Storytime Themes

- Tickle My Funny Bone
- Sibling Silliness
- Let's Do Lunch

The Rainstorm

One gray day, the rain came down. It started out gently, pit, pitter, pat. The rain came down harder, tatta tatta tatta. The thunder rolled far away, mmmmow. Playful plops came in dollops, drop, slop, splash. The cloud yawned, the storm waned, the slop slowed until the puddles filled, the breeze stilled and the stream spilled. It's gurgling washed over the lawn.

The storm gone, little noses twitched, sniffing the scent of summer. Little feet itched to skip and scamper across grass. The acres washed in the new warm rays from the peeking sun, invited creatures to creep out of their shelters and play.

Mouse first, then mole and muskrat made tiny tracks in the mud. Chickadee shook, and shiny droplets flew from damp feathers. Rabbit romped through wet weeds.

The trees shook their newly washed leaves. The bees dabbed at newly washed blossoms. The lark proclaimed the meadow, clean, clean, clean.

Notes on Telling the Story

Coach the children to use finger tapping and gentle patting to make the sound of the rainstorm in the beginning. As the rain increases, clapping and foot tapping can provide the sound of big splashes and rolling thunder.

Related Storytime Themes

- Clean and Neat
- It's Raining, It's Pouring

Picnic

Pig and Bear went for a picnic. Pig brought a jug of lemonade and a bag of red apples. Bear carried a loaf of bread and a jar of honey. They walked to a meadow full of wildflowers and decided it was the perfect spot to eat their lunch. Bear curled up on a soft patch of grass. Pig perched on a smooth, round rock.

The very minute they sat down, they heard tiny voices.

"Picnic places are not free. You must pay. Pay the fee!"

Bear stood up and looked around. There was no one to be seen. "Let's eat," he said. Breaking off a chunk of bread, he dipped it in honey and gave it to Pig. Then he broke off a piece for himself. Bear licked drizzling honey from his paws and sat down to eat.

The very minute he sat down, they heard tiny voices.

"Picnic places are not free. You must pay. Pay the fee!"

Bear stood up and looked around. He looked high and he looked low. There was no one to be seen. "Let's eat," he said. Pig rubbed an apple until it was shiny. He stood up and gave it to Bear. Then he rubbed an apple for himself. Pig took a big sniff of the sweet-smelling apple and both he and Bear sat down to eat.

The very minute they sat down, they heard tiny voices.

"Picnic places are not free. You must pay. Pay the fee!"

Bear stood up and looked around. He looked left and he looked right. There was no one to be seen. "Let's eat," he said.

Even before he sat down, they heard tiny voices.

"Picnic places are not free. You must pay. Pay the fee!"

Pig stood up and looked around. He looked over and he looked under. At last he saw them. Under a rock, the very rock he was sitting on, Pig found a swarm of picnic ants. The ants marched in single file right up to Pig and Bear, shaking their tiny fists and calling in their tiny voices,

"Picnic places are not free. You must pay. Pay the fee!"

Pig understood. He opened the jug of lemonade and poured a little puddle on the ground. The ants surrounded the tasty puddle and began to slurp. In almost no time, they slurped the puddle dry. The ants marched in single file back under their rock, singing in happy, tiny voices, "Picnic places are not free. You paid! You paid the fee."

Pig handed the jug of lemonade to Bear. "Thanks," said Bear, taking a sip. Then they both sat down and finished their picnic.

Notes on Telling the Story

The first time you say the phrase, "Picnic places are not free. You must pay. Pay the fee!" use a gesture such as cupping hands around your mouth. Then each time the phrase repeats, make the gesture and pause briefly to let the children know that they can say this phrase with you.

Related Storytime Themes

- Pigs Are Smart
- Bear Rally
- Let's Go!

A Little Train

A little train chugged along the track, singing, "Chugga, chugga. Toot, toot. Here I go, to the top of the mountain covered in snow. I bring mittens and hats and coats so all the little children will be warm as toast."

The train chugged along the track, chugga, chugga, toot, toot. Until suddenly, screech! It put on the brakes. There was a cow on the track. The cow asked, "May I come along? I'm tired of the meadow. I want to see the world."

The little train said, "Climb onboard. Here we go, to the top of the mountain covered in snow. I bring mittens and hats and coats so all the little children will be warm as toast."

The train chugged along the track, chugga, chugga, toot, toot. Until, once again, screech! It put on the brakes. There was a dog on the track. The dog asked, "May I come along? I'm too old for hunting now. I want to see the world."

The little train said, "Climb onboard. Here we go, to the top of the mountain covered in snow. I bring mittens and hats and coats so all the little children will be warm as toast."

The train chugged along the track, chugga, chugga, toot, toot. Soon it came to the foot of the mountain. The train began to climb. Chugga, chugga, toot, toot. Chugga, chugga, chugga, whoa! This part of the track was very steep. The little train could not climb any more.

"Let me help," said the cow. She got behind the train and started to push. She pushed, and she pushed until the train was over the steep part of the track.

The train said, "Climb onboard. Here we go, to the top of the mountain covered in snow. I bring mittens and hats and coats so all the little children will be warm as toast."

The train chugged along the track, chugga, chugga, toot, toot. Soon it came to thick white fog. The train chugged along, but the fog was so thick the train was afraid. "If I jump the track in this fog, the little children will not get their warm mittens and coats," said the train.

"Let me help," said the dog. He went to the front of the train and began to howl. He howled and howled until the fog parted enough for the moonlight to show the way.

The train said, "Climb onboard. Here we go, to the top of the mountain covered in snow. I bring mittens and hats and coats so all the little children will be warm as toast."

The train chugged along the track, chugga, chugga, toot, toot. After a long, long while, the train came to a village at the top of the mountain. All along the tracks at the train station, children waved and cheered. They soon put on the mittens, hats and coats and had a snowball fight. The cow used her tail to brush the snow from all of the sidewalks. The dog pulled a sled and gave the children rides.

Finally, the train said, "Climb onboard. Here we go. What we will see I do not know."

So the cow and the dog climbed on to the train. They waved to the children as the train pulled away from the station and chugged along the track, chugga, chugga, toot, toot.

Notes on Telling the Story

When you say the phrase "chugga, chugga, toot, toot," make circles with your hands to simulate the wheels of the train, and pretend to pull the whistle. Each time you do these gestures, encourage the children to do them with you and repeat the phrase with you also.

Related Storytime Themes

- Traveling Cows
- Talented Dogs
- Traveling by Train
- Warm as Toast

Storytime Themes

Clean and Neat

In honor of Organize Your Home Day, the first Monday in January.

Before Sharing Books

Bring an assortment of objects and some containers. Ask the children to match up the correct objects and containers. Try some funny ones such as: Do the socks belong in the grocery bag? Does the crayon belong in the laundry basket? (Suggested objects: apple, sock, box of cereal, ball, shirt, puzzle, crayon, teddy bear. Suggested containers: laundry basket, paper grocery bag, toy box.)

Rest Activities

Song

"Everything Has A Place"
(Sung to the tune: "A Hunting We Will Go")
My smile goes on my face.
My smile goes on my face.
Everything has a place.
My smile goes on my face.

Repeat with additional verses:
My hair goes on my head.
My hands go on my arms.

Fingerplay

Five Little Toys
Five little toys on the bedroom floor,
(Hold up five fingers.)
I'm not playing with them any more.
(Shake head, no.)
I picked one up and put it away.
(Pantomime picking up toy.)
I'll play with it another day. *(Nod head, yes.)*
Repeat with four, three, two and one.

Action Rhyme

I Clean My House
I clean my house with a vacuum.
Vroom, vroom, vroom.
(Pantomime vacuuming.)
That is the way I clean my house.
Vroom, vroom, vroom.

I clean my house with a duster.
(Pantomime dusting.)
Wiggle, wiggle, wiggle.
That is the way I clean my house.
Wiggle, wiggle, wiggle.

I clean my house with a sponge.
(Pantomime wiping.)
Squish, squish, squish.
That is the way I clean my house.
Squish, squish, squish.

Books to Share

Cousins, Lucy. *Maisy Cleans Up*. Candlewick Press, 2002. Maisy the mouse and her friend Charley clean her house together and then treat themselves to cupcakes.

Lillie, Patricia. *Everything Has a Place*. Greenwillow Books, 1993. Text and pictures assign a cow to a barn, a dish to a cupboard, a family to a house and other things to their place.

Mahoney, Daniel J. *The Saturday Escape*. Houghton Mifflin, 2002. Three friends feel guilty about going to story hour at the library instead of cleaning their rooms as their parents asked them to do.

Wallace, Nancy Elizabeth. *Count Down to Clean Up*. Houghton Mifflin, 2001. Rabbits from one to ten get ready to help clean up.

Good Worker Badge

I'm A
Good Worker

Directions

Copy and cut out a badge for each child. Use a hole punch to make holes at the small circles. At storytime, have the children color their badge. Cut yarn for each child approximately 28" in length, and tie the ends in the holes so the child can wear the badge around his or her neck. Adjust the length to fit the child.

 This craft takes 10 minutes to complete if the badges are precut.

My Favorite Things

In honor of Hunt for Happiness Week, the third full week in January. This is a week to encourage children to discover more happy moments in their everyday experiences.

Before Sharing Books

Bring some of your favorite things to display. Choose objects that can be used with fun everyday activities. As you show each thing, talk about the activity you enjoy doing. For example, "I enjoy going for a walk wearing these comfortable shoes. I enjoy taking pictures with this camera. I enjoy putting together a puzzle."

Rest Activities

Song

"Do You Like?"

(Sung to the tune: "Muffin Man")
Do you like to take a walk,
Take a walk, take a walk?
Do you like to take a walk?
I like to do that, too.
Repeat with: twirl around, call a friend, climb a tree, eat your lunch, etc.

"If You're Happy"

If you're happy and you know it, clap your hands.
If you're happy and you know it, clap your hands.
If you're happy and you know it,
Then your face will surely show it.
If you're happy and you know it, clap your hands.
Repeat with: tap your feet, shout hurray, etc.

Fingerplay

Two Best Friends

Two best friends went out to play.
(Hold up index finger on each hand.)
One named Jeff and one named Jay.
(Wiggle each finger.)
Run home, Jeff. Run home, Jay.
(Place hands behind back.)
Come back, Jeff. Come back, Jay.
(Bring hands to front again.)

Books to Share

Creech, Sharon. *A Fine, Fine School.* HarperCollins, 2001. When a principal loves his school so much that he wants the children to attend classes every day of the year, it is up to his students to show him free time is a good thing, too.

Gershator, Phillis and David. *Greetings, Sun.* DK Publishing, 1998. Throughout the day, children greet the sun, the breeze, their breakfasts, their school and all the other large and small sights that they encounter.

MacLean, Christine Kole. *Even Firefighters Hug Their Moms.* Dutton, 2002. An imaginative boy pretends to be a firefighter, policeman, construction worker and other busy people, but he realizes that it is important to take time to give his mom a hug.

Smothers, Ethel Footman. *Auntee Edna.* William B. Eerdmans Publishing Company, 2001. Although at first Tokee is unhappy having to spend the day with her old-fashioned Auntee Edna, she soon discovers her aunt is full of good ideas for fun, from baking teacakes to putting paper rollers in their hair.

Spinelli, Eileen. *In My New Yellow Shirt.* Henry Holt & Company, 2001. A boy wears his new yellow shirt and is transformed in his imagination into a duck, lion, daffodil, trumpet and other things.

Bee Happy

BEE HAPPY!

Directions
Copy the bee and flower for each child and cut out.
At storytime, have the children color them. Then
use a glue stick to paste the bee on the flower.

 **This craft takes 10 minutes
to complete if all parts are
precut.**

I Like to Share

In honor of Lost Penny Day, February 12, Abraham Lincoln's birthday. This is a day to gather up the pennies in drawers and jars about your home and give them to a worthy charity.

Before Sharing Books

Set out a variety of coin banks. Choose one of the banks and put ten pennies in it, allowing the children to help you count them. Tell the children what you plan to do with the pennies in the bank when it is full. You may talk about saving the pennies to buy something you have been wanting. Be sure to suggest to the children that you might share the pennies with a friend, or give them to a charity.

Rest Activities

Song

"Share Your Lunch"

(Sung to the tune: "Row, Row, Row Your Boat")
Share, share, share your lunch.
Share your cookies, too.
Some for you and some for me.
A nice thing to do.

Fingerplay

Shiny Penny
Here in my hand I have something nice,
(Make a fist.)
Shiny, smooth and round.
It's not candy to eat. *(Fingers touch lips.)*
It's not a little ball. *(Pretend to bounce a ball.)*
It's not a black bug
That likes to crawl.
(Walk fingers on arm.)

Here in my hand, can you guess what I have?
(Make a fist.)
It's a penny that I found.
(Open hand.)

Action Rhyme

A Kiss from Me
I touch my knees.
I touch my toes.
I touch my head.
I touch my nose.
I clap three times,
One, two, three.
I jump three times,
One, two, three.
I turn around slowly,
As slow as can be
And I blow a kiss!
It's a kiss from me.

Books to Share

Dyer, Sarah. *Five Little Fiends.* Bloomsbury, 2002. Each of the five little fiends claims his favorite part of the world—the sun, the moon, the sea, the sky and the land. They soon decide that one of these things is no good without the others.

Napoli, Donna Jo and Richard Tchen. *How Hungry Are You?* Simon & Schuster, 2001. A pink rabbit and a green frog plan a picnic of sandwiches and juice. A monkey, a blackbird and others join them, each bringing something to share.

Pacilio, V. J. *Ling Cho and His Three Friends.* Farrar, Straus and Giroux, 2000. Ling Cho is a prosperous farmer who comes up with a plan to help each of his less prosperous neighbors.

Wood, Audrey. *Jubal's Wish.* Blue Sky Press, 2000. Jubal Bullfrog has a picnic to share. When his friends are too busy to go with him, he makes a wish that his friends could be happy. A wizard grants his wish but warns him, you never know how wishes will turn out.

I Like To Share Lunch Bag

I like to share!

Directions

Copy the smiling face and conversation bubble for each child and cut out. At storytime, have the child color the smiling face. Using a glue stick, let the child glue the smiling face and conversation bubble to a small paper bag. Encourage the children to pack the bag with food to share with a friend or family member.

 This craft takes 5 minutes to complete if all parts are precut.

Traveling Cows

In honor of the anniversary of the first cow milked while flying in an airplane, February 18, 1930.

Rest Activities

Song

"Spotted Cow, Spotted Cow"
(Sung to the tune: "Pussycat, Pussycat")
Spotted cow, spotted cow, where have you been?
I went on vacation. I traveled by train.
Spotted cow, spotted cow, did you have fun?
I swam in the ocean and tanned in the sun.

Rhyme

Hey, Diddle Diddle
(Traditional)
Hey, diddle diddle,
The cat and the fiddle,
The cow jumped over the moon.
The little dog laughed to see such a sport,
And the dish ran away with the spoon.

Fingerplay

Cow On a Walk
(May use cow finger puppet.)
A brown cow went for a walk,
On a sunny day.
She walked up a hill,
(Walk two fingers on arm, going up.)
And down a hill,
(Walk two fingers on arm, going down.)
And up a hill,
(Repeat above actions.)
And down a hill,
And up a hill,
And down a hill.
She stopped to look around.
(Fingers stop walking.)
She nibbled a bite of grass.
(Fingers kneel down on arm.)
She lay down for a rest.
(Lay hand on arm.)
"Time to go home," she said.
(Make hand stand up again.)
So she walked up a hill,
(Walk two fingers on arm, going up.)
And down a hill,
(Walk two fingers on arm, going down.)
And up a hill,
(Repeat above actions.)
And down a hill,
And up a hill,
And down a hill.
Until she got home.
(Fingers stop walking.)
"Traveling is nice," she said,
"But home is best."

Books to Share

Johnson, Paul Brett. *The Cow Who Wouldn't Come Down*. Orchard Books, 1993. Miss Rosemary's cow, Gertrude, insists on flying through the air.

Kent, Jack. *Mrs. Mooley*. Golden Books, 2002. Mrs. Mooley is inspired by a book of nursery rhymes and decides to jump over the moon.

Smith, Mary Ann. *Cappuccina Goes to Town*. Kids Can Press, 2002. Cappuccina thinks it would be more fun to be a human than a cow. She heads to town for a shopping spree.

Wheeler, Lisa. *Sailor Moo: Cow at Sea*. Simon & Schuster, 2002. Moo leaves the farm and goes on an adventure at sea where she is thrown overboard. She is rescued by manatees and is taken to a pirate ship.

Flying Cow

Directions
Copy the cow for each child and cut out. At storytime, have the children color the cow. Tape a 24" piece of yarn to the back of the plane just behind the propeller. The children can hold onto the string and wave their hand, making the flying cow soar through the air.

 This craft takes 5 minutes to complete if all parts are precut.

Pigs Are Smart

In honor of National Pig Day, March 1.

Before Sharing Books

Ask the children to think of as many words as they can to describe a pig. Here are some ideas: cute, pink, fat, noisy, muddy, smelly, big, hairy and smart.

Rest Activities

Songs

"Did You Ever See a Piggy?"
(Sung to the tune: "Did You Ever See a Lassie?")
Did you ever see a piggy, a piggy, a piggy,
Did you ever see a piggy,
Riding a bike?
Riding and riding and riding and riding,
Did you ever see a piggy riding a bike?

Repeat with: sailing a boat, playing a horn, baking a pie.

"Do the Hokey Piggy"
(Sung to the tune: "Hokey Pokey")
Put your funny nose in, put your funny nose out.
Put your funny nose in and shake it all about.
Do the Hokey Piggy and turn yourself around.
That's what it's all about.

Repeat with: put your pointy ears in, put your curly tail in, put your piggy self in.

Rhyme

Smelly Pig
I'm a smelly pig in a big mud hole,
My brothers are smelly, too.
But, oh, my goodness, bless my soul,
We are not as smelly as you.
NO WAY.
We are not as smelly as you.

Books to Share

Beil, Karen Magnuson. *A Cake All for Me!* Holiday House, 1998. Piggy mixes and bakes a cake that he plans to eat all by himself. The steps to making the cake follow a counting rhyme.

Brown, Margaret Wise. *The Good Little Bad Little Pig.* Hyperion, 2002. Peter asks for a good little bad little pig, which he bathes and feeds by himself. When his parents complain that it is dirty and noisy, Peter convinces them that it is a lovable pig.

Hobbie, Holly. *Toot and Puddle: Top of the World.* Little, Brown and Company, 2002. When Toot goes for a walk and doesn't come back by dinnertime, Puddle goes looking for him. He tries to think just like his best friend to track him down.

McPhail, David. *Those Can-Do Pigs.* Penguin, 1996. These pigs can do just about everything, including fending off shark attacks and rocketing to the moon.

Smiling Pig

face

ears

head

lower body

Directions
Copy a set of pig pieces for each child and cut out. At story-time, help the children glue the head and lower body together, forming two rings. Glue the head on the body. Next, have the children glue the face and ears to the head.

 This craft takes 10 minutes to complete if all parts are precut.

It's Raining, It's Pouring

In honor of National Umbrella Month during March.

Before Sharing Books

Lead the children in making the sound of a gentle rain by tapping lightly on your lap. Beat on a drum, simulating the sound of thunder. Ask everyone to tap faster and harder, making the sound of a hard rain. Slowly, the rain decreases and the tapping slows. Now ask them to take a deep breath of the fresh smell of rain.

Rest Activities

Song

"It's Raining Out"

(Sung to the tune: "A Hunting We Will Go")
It's raining out today.
It's raining out today.
I can't go out and play.
It's raining out today.
The rain is stopping now.
The rain is stopping now.
Now I can go outside.
The rain is stopping now.

Action Rhymes

A Stormy Day

Way up in the sky, *(Reach arms over head.)*
Clouds are floating by. *(Wave arms.)*
The wind blows my hair, *(Touch hair.)*
And whispers in my ear. *(Touch ears.)*
Plop, plop, plop. *(Fingers wiggle.)*
Hear the raindrops. *(Touch the floor.)*
Run! Run inside. *(Run in place.)*
Watch the storm go by.
(Hands by face, as if looking out a window.)

What Should I Wear?

What should I wear on a stormy day?
(Shrug shoulders.)
What should I wear today?
I'll wear a raincoat.
(Pretend to put on coat.)
I'll wear my boots.
(Pretend to put on boots.)
I'll open up my umbrella, too.
(Pretend to open an umbrella.)
Now I'll be dry on a stormy day.
(Smile and nod head.)
Now I'll be dry today.

Books to Share

Crimi, Carolyn. *Tessa's Tip-Tapping Toes.* Orchard Books, 2002. Tessa the mouse loves to dance. Oscar the cat loves to sing. Tessa and Oscar meet one rainy night, and pretty soon everyone is hip-hopping and sing-songing with them.

Gorbachev, Valeri. *One Rainy Day.* Philomel, 2001. Goat asks his sopping wet friend Pig, "Why didn't you hide under a tree?" "I did," he replies, and begins a hilarious explanation.

Kurtz, Jane. *Rain Romp.* HarperCollins, 2002. On a gray, dreary day, a child feels very angry. Stomping in the rain puddles makes her feel much better.

Mitchell, Marianne. *Gullywasher Gulch.* Boyds Mills Press, 2004. Eb the prospector saves tools, lumber, nails and gold nuggets in his shack high above the desert town of Dry Gulch.

Shannon, David. *The Rain Came Down.* Scholastic, 2000. On Saturday morning the rain comes down, which makes the chickens squawk and everyone else very crabby. When the rain stops, the sun comes out and the air smells sweet, changing everything.

Rainy Blossom Frog

Directions

Copy the rainy blossom and the frog for each child and cut out. At storytime, have the children color the blossom and the frog. Tape a green pipe cleaner to the blossom, forming a stem. Tape the other end of the pipe cleaner to the back of the frog. Curve the pipe cleaner slightly, so the blossom is over the frog's head and the raindrops are dripping on him.

 This craft takes 10 minutes to complete if all parts are precut.

Tickle My Funny Bone

In honor of National Humor Month during April.

Before Sharing Books

Tell the children that before you can read stories today, you have to put on your silly shoes, your silly coat, your silly hat, etc. Pantomime putting them on, or bring real clothing to put on. The last thing you have to do to be ready for stories today is to find out if anyone in the room has a funny bone. Take a large feather and tickle first yourself, then some of the children. Be sure to giggle a lot. Now that the funny bone has been found, you may begin the stories.

Rest Activities

Songs

"Did You Ever Have a Giggle?"
(Sung to the tune: "Did You Ever See a Lassie?")
Did you ever have a giggle, a giggle, a giggle,
Did you ever have a giggle,
That would not come out?
Try this way and that way.
Try this way and that way.
Did you ever have a giggle,
That would not come out?
Experiment with different styles of laughing, the sillier the better.

"I Can Make a Silly Face"
(Sung to the tune: "Mary Had a Little Lamb")
I can make a silly face,
Silly face, silly face.
I can make a silly face,
Because it makes you laugh.

Action Rhyme

Jump, Jump, Jump
Jump, jump, jump. *(Jump in place.)*
Turn around. *(Turn around in place.)*
Hands go up. *(Raise hands above head.)*
Hands go down. *(Lower hands.)*
Wiggle your fingers. *(Wiggle fingers.)*
Wiggle your toes. *(Point to feet and wiggle toes.)*
Wiggle your middle. *(Wiggle torso.)*
Wiggle your nose. *(Use finger to wiggle nose.)*

Take a deep breath. *(Breathe in.)*
Blow a big, big bubble.
(Simulate bubble with hands. Clap when bubble pops.)
Now sit down. *(Quickly sit down.)*
On the double!

Books to Share

Breathed, Berkeley. *Edwurd Fudwupper Fibbed Big.* Little, Brown and Company, 2000. Edwurd's little sister comes to the rescue when Edwurd's humongous fib lands him in trouble with a three-eyed alien from another galaxy.

Chwast, Seymour. *Harry, I Need You!* Houghton Mifflin, 2002. When Harry's mother calls him to get out of bed to see a surprise, he tries to imagine what it could be.

Collicott, Sharleen. *Toestomper and the Caterpillars.* Houghton Mifflin, 1999. Toestomper is the kind of big, ugly bully kids run and hide from, and his lowlife friends, the Rowdy Ruffians, are no better. So what happens when a bunch of darling baby caterpillars start following Toestomper around asking for help?

Wood, Audrey. *Silly Sally.* Harcourt, 1992. Silly Sally and her zany new companions parade to town, dancing jigs with pigs and singing tunes with loons, but things come to a halt when they are joined by a sheep and they all fall asleep.

Funny Bone Bookmark

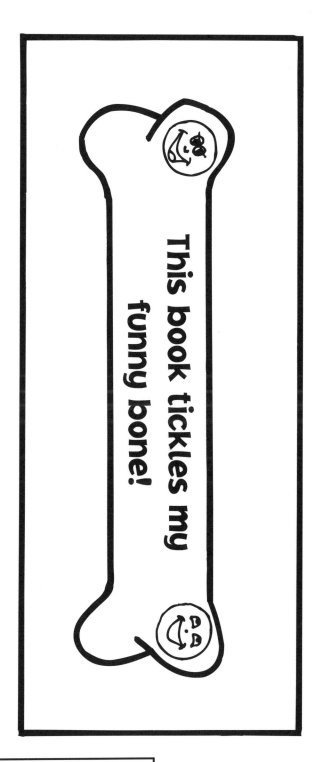

The bone reads: This book tickles my funny bone!

Directions
Copy the bookmark for each child and cut out. At storytime, have the children color the bookmark.
Optional: Give the children smiley face stickers to put on the bookmark after they color it.

 This craft takes 5 minutes to compete if all parts are precut.

Sibling Silliness

In honor of National Sibling Day, April 10. This is a day to honor all brothers and sisters.

Before Sharing Books

Bring two teddy bears to storytime. Introduce them as brother and sister. Describe what each one likes to eat for breakfast, games each one likes to play, and what each one likes to sleep with. For example: Garth likes scrambled eggs for breakfast. Gretchen likes oatmeal with honey. Garth likes to make mud pies. Gretchen likes to paint pictures. Garth sleeps with a soft blanket. Gretchen sleeps with her stuffed bunny.

Rest Activities

Song

"Ten Little Brothers"

(Sung to the tune: "Ten Little Indians")
(Hold up fingers one at a time.)
One little, two little, three little brothers.
Four little, five little, six little brothers.
Seven little, eight little, nine little brothers.
Ten in the family.
Repeat, substituting sisters for brothers.

Action Rhyme

Big Brother
My big brother is very tall. *(Hands over head.)*
He plays chess and basketball.
(Pretend to dribble ball.)
For breakfast he eats toast and jelly. *(Pretend to eat.)*
His shoes are big and his socks are smelly.
(Hold nose.)
He carries a backpack to school. *(Point to shoulders.)*
His clothes and hair are very cool.
(Touch hair and smile.)
I'm getting bigger every day. *(Stand up tall.)*
I'll be as big as my brother some day. *(Point to self.)*

Fingerplay

Two Little Sisters
Two little sisters went out to play.
(Hold up two fingers.)
What are they going to do today?
(Wiggle the fingers.)
They climbed up to the top of a tree.
(Raise hands high.)
They looked around and what did they see?
(Turn hands left and right.)
The ice cream truck was coming down the street,
So they climbed back down and said,
(Hands down.)
"Let's get a treat!"
(Rub tummy.)

Books to Share

Cutler, Jane. *Darcy and Gran Don't Like Babies*. Farrar, Straus and Giroux, 2002. Darcy and Gran are not happy about the idea of a new baby coming, but they change their minds after the birth.

Dealey, Erin. *Goldie Locks Has Chicken Pox*. Simon & Schuster, 2002. When Goldie Locks comes down with chicken pox, she is teased by her brother and is unable to visit with Bo Peep, Little Red and other friends.

Gay, Marie-Louise. *Stella, Fairy of the Forest*. Groundwood Books, 2002. Stella and her brother Sam take a delightful walk in the forest to look for fairies.

McCullough, Sharon Pierce. *Bunbun, the Middle One*. Barefoot Books, 2001. Bunbun is younger than his brother Bennie and older than his sister Bibi. But Bunbun gets noticed because he sings the loudest and gets the dirtiest.

Numeroff, Laura. *The Chicken Sisters*. HarperCollins, 1999. Three chickens have favorite activities, but they do them badly. Violet loves to bake, but frequently fills the house with smoke. Poppy loves to knit "hats with chin straps" and "turtleneck sweaters with pompoms." Babs loves to sing even though she is often off-key.

Gretchen and Garth Bear Stick Puppets

Gretchen

Garth

Directions
Copy the bear patterns for each child and cut out. Glue a Popsicle stick to each bear. Give each child one of each bear at storytime. Have the children color their stick puppets.

 This craft takes 10 minutes to complete if all parts are precut and glued.

Rhyme Time

In honor of Mother Goose Day, May 1.

Before Sharing Books

Bring some objects or toys that illustrate your favorite rhymes. Say the rhymes as you display the object.

Examples:

* Pumpkin: "Peter Peter Pumpkin Eater"
* Shoe: "Diddle Diddle Dumpling"
* Candle: "Jack Be Nimble"
* Flowers: "Mary, Mary, Quite Contrary"

Rest Activities

Song

"I Can Say Rhymes"
(Sung to the tune: "Twinkle, Twinkle, Little Star")
Humpty Dumpty, Little Bo Peep,
Little Boy Blue is fast asleep.
Baa, Baa, Black Sheep, Jack and Jill,
Two little blackbirds sitting on a hill.
I can say them anytime,
I know lots and lots of rhymes.

Action Rhymes

Stand Up Tall
Stand up tall and touch your head.
Bend down and touch your toes instead.
Clap three times, turn around,
Wave to your neighbor and then sit down.

Eyes and Nose
Eyes and nose and ears and chin.
That's the way the rhyme begins.
Hands on head.
Hands in lap.
Shhhh! It's time for baby's nap.

Books to Share

Hague, Michael. *Teddy Bear's Mother Goose.* Henry Holt & Company, 2001. Bears take a starring role in 55 classic mother goose rhymes.

Kirk, Daniel. *Humpty Dumpty.* Putnam, 2002. While watching young King Moe's birthday parade, Humpty Dumpty falls and breaks, but the King is able to put him back together.

Montgomery, Michael. *Over the Candlestick: Classic Nursery Rhymes and the Real Stories Behind Them.*

Peachtree Publishers, 2002. Fourteen well-known nursery rhymes, along with a selection of riddles and tongue twisters, are illustrated and easy to show in large picture-book format.

Muller, Robin. *Hickory, Dickory, Dock.* Scholastic, 1994. At a special party hosted by an elegant cat, the guests go in search of a beautiful hidden clock. Based on the traditional nursery rhyme.

Humpty Dumpty Puzzle

Directions

Enlarge and copy the Humpty Dumpty picture for each child. Cut them out. Cut each picture into three or four pieces. Paper clip the pieces together, or put them in a small bag. At storytime, have the children arrange the pieces on a sheet of construction paper. Have them glue the pieces in place with a glue stick and color.

 This craft takes 10 minutes to complete if all parts are precut.

Going Visiting

In honor of Visit Your Relatives Day, May 18.

Before Sharing Books

Bring a suitcase to storytime, packed with things a child would need for an overnight visit. Bring them out one at a time and talk about why they are needed. Include such items as pajamas, toothbrush and a special toy.

Rest Activities

Song

"The Bear Went Over the Mountain"
(Traditional)
The bear went over the mountain,
The bear went over the mountain,
The bear went over the mountain,
To see what he could see.
And all that he could see,
And all that he could see,
Was the other side of the mountain.
The other side of the mountain,
The other side of the mountain,
Was all that he could see.

Action Rhyme

Staying Overnight
I'm staying overnight,
(Lay face on hand as if sleeping.)
At Grampy and Gran's.
For supper we'll all eat *(Pretend to eat.)*
Biscuits and jam.
Grampy will play *(Clap hands twice, pat legs twice.)*
A game with me.
Gran will read stories,
(Hands together forming a book.)
One, two, three. *(Hold up three fingers.)*
After my bath, *(Pretend to wash.)*
They will tuck me in, *(Pat sides of body.)*
And cuddle the blanket,
(Pretend to hold blanket to chin.)
Around my chin.

Fingerplay

Who's At the Door?
Knock, knock, knock. *(Hold up a fist, knock.)*
Who's at the door?
All my cousins.
One, two, three, four!
(Open hand, count four fingers.)

Books to Share

Ada, Alma Flor. *I Love Saturdays y Domingos.* Simon & Schuster, 2001. A young girl enjoys the similarities and the differences between her English-speaking and Spanish-speaking grandparents.

Carlstrom, Nancy White. *Guess Who's Coming, Jesse Bear?* Simon & Schuster, 2002. When Jesse Bear finds out that his older cousin is coming for a visit, he's not happy about it; but things turn out differently from what he imagined.

Jones, Rebecca C. *Great Aunt Martha.* Penguin, 1995. A young girl cannot watch television, dance or play with the dog because her parents think that a visiting great-aunt needs her rest.

St. James, Synthia. *Sunday.* Albert Whitman, 1996. Twin girls spend a typical Sunday eating breakfast, going to church and visiting their grandparents.

Staying Overnight Coloring Sheet

Good night. Sleep tight.
I like staying overnight.

Directions
Copy the coloring sheet for each child. Have the children color them at storytime.

 This craft takes 5 minutes to complete.

Talented Dogs

In honor of Take Your Dog to Work Day, the first Friday after Father's Day.

Before Sharing Books

Bring some toy dogs to storytime. Make them do some tricks, such as sit, stay, play dead, roll over and speak.

Rest Activities

Songs

"My Dog"

(Sung to the tune: "Twinkle, Twinkle, Little Star")
My dog likes to chase his tail.
He can beg and bark and wail.
He can fetch a rubber ball.
He comes running when I call.
My dog is a friend to me.
He's the best; it's plain to see.

"If You're Happy"

(Adapted Traditional)
If you're happy and you know it give a bark.
(Bark, bark.)
If you're happy and you know it give a bark.
(Bark, bark.)
If you're happy and you know it,
A dog just has to show it.
If you're happy and you know it give a bark.
(Bark, bark.)
Repeat with: turn around, wag your tail, do all three.

Fingerplay

Spot and Mack

Two little dogs were playing out back.
(Each hand forms a dog head.)
One named Spot and one named Mack.
(Left hand barks, right hand barks.)
Spot dug a hole.
(Left hand digs.)
Mack chased a ball.
(Right hand moves forward quickly.)
They both came running when they heard me call.
(Shake both hands.)

Books to Share

Edwards, Pamela Duncan. *Muldoon*. Hyperion, 2002. Muldoon, a dog, serves the West family with humorous results.

Flather, Lisa. *Ten Silly Dogs: A Countdown Story*. Orchard Books, 1999. Ten silly dogs go running in the park. One by one they leave the pack, until one very dirty dog is left alone, but not for long.

Freymann, Saxton and Joost Elffers. *Dog Food*. Scholastic, 2002. Dog figures carved out of different fruits and vegetables "act out" such phrases as "bad dog," "sick as a dog" and "doggy bag."

Mahy, Margaret. *Dashing Dog!* HarperCollins, 2002. Rhyming verse tells the story of a "cleaned up and curlicued" poodle on a seaside jaunt with his human family. This dashing dog is soon a mess, because he likes nothing better than to play with seagulls and seaweed. When baby Betty wanders away, the dashing dog dashes off to rescue her.

Newman, Leslea. *Dogs, Dogs, Dogs*. Simon & Schuster, 2002. A counting book featuring dogs engaged in various activities, from walking through the city all alone to slurping up a fallen ice cream cone.

Talented Dogs Coloring Sheet

Directions
Copy the talented dogs coloring sheet for each child. At storytime, have them color it.

 This craft takes 5 minutes to complete.

Happy Birthday

In honor of the anniversary of the song "Happy Birthday to You," composed by Mildred J. Hill on June 27, 1859.

Before Sharing Books

Decorate the storytime room with balloons, streamers and party hats. Ask the children if they have ever had a birthday party. Ask if they have ever been to a birthday party. Tell them that today is a party for the song "Happy Birthday to You." Sing the song together. You may wish to bring cupcakes or other treats for each child.

Rest Activities

Song

"Oh, Birthday Cake"
(Sung to the tune: "Oh, Christmas Tree")
Oh, birthday cake, oh, birthday cake,
You have such pretty frosting.
Oh, birthday cake, oh, birthday cake,
You have such pretty frosting.
I see the candles shining bright.
I'll make a wish when I blow them out.
Oh, birthday cake, oh, birthday cake,
You have such pretty frosting.

Action Rhyme

My Birthday
I wash my face. *(Pretend to wash face.)*
I comb my hair. *(Pretend to comb hair.)*
I put on clean clothes. *(Pretend to dress.)*
I go downstairs. *(Walk in place.)*
I put on a party hat. *(Pretend to put on hat.)*
I have ice cream in a dish. *(Hands form a dish.)*
I blow out the candles *(Blow.)*
And make a wish.

Fingerplay

Three Balloons
Three balloons with pretty strings,
(Pretend to hold the balloon strings.)
Yellow, pink and green.
Untie the strings, they fly away,
(Pretend to release the balloons.)
One, two, three.
(Watch them fly away.)

Books to Share

Jessup, Harley. *What's Alice Up To?* Viking, 1997. A young girl acts mysteriously all day as she prepares a surprise for her dog.

Jonell, Lynne. *It's My Birthday, Too!* Penguin, 2001. Christopher would rather have a dog than a little brother who ruins his birthday parties, but when his brother begins to act like a puppy Christopher has a change of heart.

Offen, Hilda. *Elephant Pie.* Penguin, 1993. The Snipper-Snapper family orders a birthday pie from Mrs. Elephant.

Uff, Caroline. *Happy Birthday, Lulu!* Walker & Co., 2000. On her birthday, a young girl receives hugs, cards, telephone calls, presents and a party.

Wallace, John. *Tiny Rabbit Goes to a Birthday Party.* Holiday House, 2000. Tiny Rabbit is worried about going to Blue Mouse's birthday party because he has never been to a party before, but then he finds himself enjoying the games and the food.

Birthday Hat

Directions
Copy the birthday circle and cut out. Cut construction paper headbands for each child, 1½" x 20". Glue the birthday circle to the center of the paper headband. At storytime, have the children color their birthday circles. Adjust the headband to fit each child and fasten with tape.

 This craft takes 10 minutes to complete if all parts are precut.

The Moon and Other Wonders

In honor of Moon Day, the anniversary of humankind's first landing on the moon, July 20, 1969.

Before Sharing Books

Show a poster of the moon or a picture from a book. Tell the children that the moon is very far away. Once, some brave men flew in a rocket ship to the moon. They were called astronauts.

Rest Activities

Song

"The Moon Is a Wonder"
(Sung to the tune: "It's a Gift to be Simple")
The moon is a wonder.
The moon is a delight.
The moon gives off a soft glow at night.
From my bedroom window,
I look up at the moon,
And I wonder if I can go there soon.
If the children are old enough, try singing this song as a round.

Action Rhymes

A Small Step and a Giant Leap
Take a small step on the moon. *(Small step.)*
A small step for man.
Look around at the moonscape,
(Look left and right.)
And take a small step again. *(Small step.)*

Take a giant leap on the moon. *(Jump.)*
A giant leap for mankind.
Then blast off in your rocket ship,
(Hands over head, touching.)
And leave the moon behind.

Moon Craters
A tiny crater, *(Hands form a circle.)*
A bigger crater, *(Move hands out to wider circle.)*
A great big crater I see. *(Arms form large circle.)*
Watch me jump over the craters,
One, two, three. *(Jump three times.)*

Books to Share

Carle, Eric. *Papa, Please Get the Moon for Me*. Simon & Schuster, 1991. Monica's father fulfills her request for the moon by taking it down after it is small enough to carry, but it continues to change in size.

DuBurke, Randy. *The Moon Ring*. Chronicle Books, 2002. One hot night, Maxine goes on a wild adventure thanks to the magic of the blue moon.

Haddon, Mark. *The Sea of Tranquility*. HarperCollins, 1996. A man remembers his boyhood fascination with the moon and the night people first bounced through the dust in the Sea of Tranquility.

Yaccarino, Dan. *Zoom! Zoom! Zoom! I'm Off to the Moon!* Scholastic, 1997. A boy gets in a spaceship and takes a dangerous but exciting trip to the moon.

Moon Picture

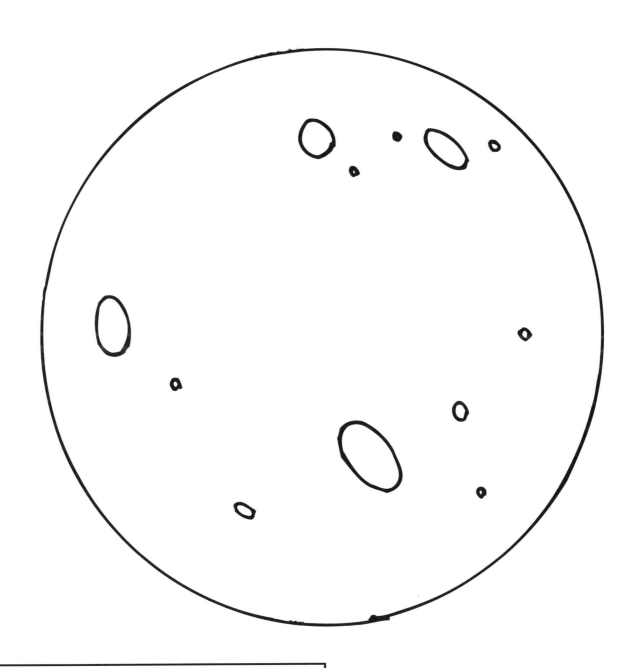

Directions
Copy the moon drawing for each child and cut out. At storytime, give each child a black or dark blue sheet of construction paper. Have the children glue the moon drawing on the construction paper using a glue stick. You may also give them star stickers to add to the picture.

 This craft takes 5 minutes to complete if all parts are precut.

Be Kind to Carrots

In honor of National Salad Week, the last week in July.

Before Sharing Books

Bring in some produce from a farmer's market. Talk about your favorite vegetables and ask the children to tell you their favorites.

Rest Activities

Songs

"Be Kind to Carrots"
(Sung to the tune: "Away In a Manger")
Be kind to your carrots.
Be kind to your beans.
Be kind to cucumbers.
Be kind to all greens.
Be kind to your squashes
And radishes, too.
For veggies will always,
Be so good for you.

"Oats, Peas, Beans and Barley"
(Traditional)
Oats, peas, beans and barley grow.
Oats, peas, beans and barley grow.
Nor you, nor I, nor anyone knows,
How oats, peas, beans and barley grow.

"Making a Salad"
(Sung to the tune: "Here We Go 'Round")
This is the way to tear the lettuce,
Tear the lettuce, tear the lettuce.
This is the way to tear the lettuce,
To make a lovely salad.
Repeat with: chop the tomatoes, grate the carrots, pour the dressing, etc.

Books to Share

Barrett, Judi. *Old MacDonald Had an Apartment House.* Simon & Schuster, 1998. Mr. MacDonald, an apartment super, turns his building into a four-story farm with hot and cold running sweet potato vines, ceiling carrots, carpets of cabbages and other farm produce and animals, prompting all the tenants to move out.

Hall, Zoe. *The Surprise Garden.* Scholastic, 1998. After sowing unmarked seeds, three youngsters wait expectantly for their garden to grow.

Keller, Holly. *Cecil's Garden.* HarperCollins, 2002. After seeing how arguing affects the other animals, Cecil figures out how to plant a garden that he and his friends can all enjoy.

Lester, Mike. *A is for Salad.* Putnam, 2002. Each letter of the alphabet is presented in an unusual way, such as "A is for salad" showing an alligator eating a bowl of greens.

Vegetable Rubbings

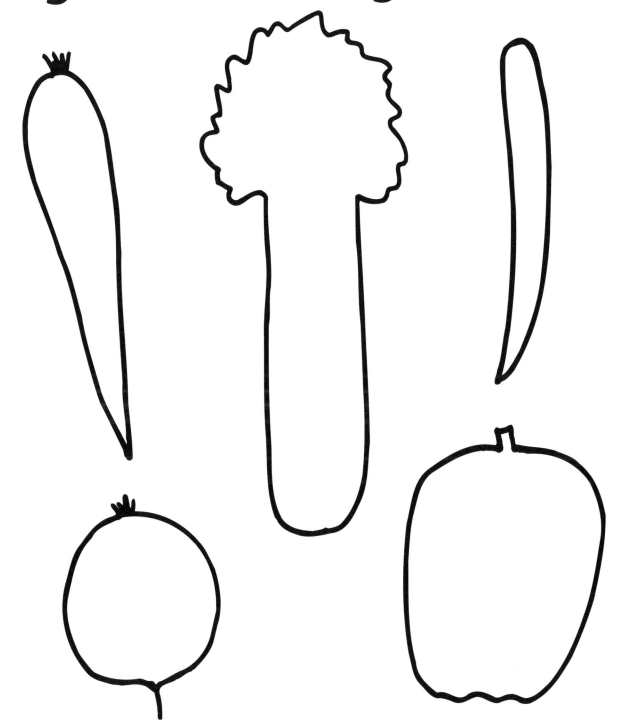

Directions
Copy the vegetable pictures on stiff paper and cut out. At storytime, give each child a sheet of newsprint and a peeled crayon. Have the child put a vegetable cut-out under the newsprint, then rub the crayon over it until the image of the vegetable shows. The child may repeat, using a different vegetable shape.

 This craft takes 5 minutes to complete if all parts are precut.

Bear Rally

In honor of Amherst, Massachusett's, annual Teddy Bear Rally in August.

Before Sharing Books

You may ask the children to bring a teddy bear with them to storytime today. Allow the children to introduce their bear to the other children if they wish. Bring a bear of your own, too!

Rest Activities

Fingerplay

This Little Bear

This little bear likes honey.
(Open hand, point to little finger.)
This little bear likes fish. *(Point to ring finger.)*
This little bear likes money. *(Point to middle finger.)*
This little bear made a wish. *(Point to index finger.)*
And this little bear gives the best bear hugs.
(Point to thumb.)
Hug! Hug! Hug! *(Make a fist to hug other bears.)*

Action Rhyme

My Teddy Bear

My Teddy Bear has two round ears.
(Fists on top of head.)
My Teddy Bear has a tail. *(One fist on back.)*
My Teddy Bear likes to fly a plane.
(Arms out as if flying.)
My Teddy Bear likes to sail.
(Arms overhead to form mast, feet glide a few steps.)
My Teddy Bear has a best friend.
(Hug arms around body.)

Who is it? Can you guess? *(Shrug shoulders.)*
Do you think that friend is me? *(Point to self.)*
If you ask me, I'll say yes. *(Nod head yes.)*

Clapping Rhyme

Don't Stare at the Bear

(Clap hands on the last three words of each line.)
Once there was a bear, bear, bear,
With honey-colored hair, hair, hair.
He wore blue underwear, wear, wear,
The other bears would stare, stare, stare.

One day he went to France, France, France,
And bought a pair of pants, pants, pants.
And now he loves to dance, dance, dance,
Each time he gets a chance, chance, chance.

And now the bears don't stare, stare, stare,
At the funny little bear, bear, bear.
With honey-colored hair, hair, hair,
And bright blue underwear, wear, wear.

Books to Share

Miller, Ruth. *The Bear On the Bed*. Kids Can Press, 2002. A big brown bear chooses not to participate in campground diversions but hangs out in the cabin and on the bunk of a mortified little girl in pigtails. Some parents may groan out loud when you read the last page.

Root, Phyllis. *Oliver Finds His Way*. Candlewick Press, 2002. Oliver the bear becomes lost when he chases a leaf to the edge of the woods, but then he comes up with an idea to find his way back home.

Ryder, Joanne. *Big Bear Ball*. HarperCollins, 2002. The moon is full and all the bears are gathered together for a ball under the stars.

Rylant, Cynthia. *Bear Day*. Harcourt, 1998. A bear enjoys every moment of the day, from eating grapes in the morning to walking on the roadside to dreaming with Teddy by his side.

Teddy Bear Paper Doll

Directions
Copy the paper doll for each child. At storytime, have the children color the bear and the clothes. They may cut out the clothes and dress the bear at home.

 This craft takes 10 minutes to complete.

Traveling by Train

In honor of the completion of the Transcontinental U.S. Railway, August 15, 1870.

Before Sharing Books

Bring an assortment of cardboard boxes. Tell the children that you will make a storytime train from these boxes. Let them help you select a box to be the engine, then line up the other boxes behind it to be the cars. The last one is the caboose. Now get everyone to help you blow the train whistle, which is the signal for storytime to begin.

Rest Activities

Song

"Take A Ride"
(Sung to the tune: "Twinkle, Twinkle, Little Star")
Do you want to take a ride?
Buy a ticket, climb inside.
Now the train goes down the track,
Hear the wheels go clickety clack.
We will go a long, long way,
What a way to spend the day.

Action Rhymes

Train Ride
The whistle blows,
(Hand in air, pull down, make sound.)
I wave good-bye,
(Wave hand.)
And down the tracks we go.
(Move arms to simulate train wheels.)
Downhill we go very fast,
(Move arms faster.)
But uphill we go slow.
(Move arms slowly.)

Five Trains in the Station
Five trains in the station, ready to go.
(Hold up five fingers.)
Big ones.
(Hands over head.)
Small ones.
(Hands by knees.)
Fast and slow.
(Run in place.)
With a toot, toot, toot and a clickety clack.
(Hand in air, pull down.)
One of the trains goes down the track.
Repeat with four, three, two, one.

You may want to make five trains for a flannel board or magnet board. Remove one train from the board after each verse.

Books to Share

Brown, Margaret Wise. *Two Little Trains.* HarperCollins, 2001. Two little trains, one stream-lined, the other old-fashioned, puff, puff, puff and chug, chug, chug on their way West.

Gurney, John Steven. *Dinosaur Train.* HarperCollins, 2002. Young Jesse, a big fan of both dinosaurs and trains, is thrilled when a dinosaur who happens to be a train conductor shows up at his bedroom window.

Suen, Anastasia. *Window Music.* Penguin Putnam, 1998. Describes the trip taken by a train as it travels over hills, through valleys, past horses and orange trees until it arrives at the next station.

Train Picture

Directions

Copy the train parts on a variety of colors of paper and cut out. Paper clip the train parts together, or put them into a small bag for each child. Give each child a variety of colors. At storytime, give each child a sheet of construction paper and a glue stick. Let each child glue the train parts on the construction paper. Have them draw a train track with crayons.

 This craft takes 10 minutes to complete if all parts are precut.

Take Good Care of Your Baby

In honor of Baby Safety Month during September.

Before Sharing Books

Ask to borrow some baby toys, clothes, powder, etc., from a friend or patron with a baby. Discuss with the children why babies need these things and why we must be careful when playing with and holding babies.

Rest Activities

Song

"Baby Has a Little Hand"
(Sung to the tune: "Mary Had a Little Lamb")
Baby has a little hand, little hand, little hand.
Baby has a little hand as cute as it can be.
Repeat with: little foot, little nose, little head.

Action Rhymes

Baby's Play and My Play
Baby likes to shake his rattle,
(Hold up a fist.)
Shake, shake, shake.
(Shake fist in the air.)
I like to build with blocks.
(Put one fist on the other, repeat a few times.)
So many things I make.
(Arms out wide.)
Baby holds his rubber mouse,
(Open and close hand.)

That makes a funny squeak.
(Make a squeaking noise.)
I like to paint pictures,
(Pretend to paint.)
And play hide and seek.
(Cover eyes with hands, then uncover them.)

Holding the Baby
When I hold the baby,
(Begin by standing up. Pretend to sit.)
I sit in a chair
And hold my arms like this
(Fold arms across chest.)
And take great care.
(Pretend to rock baby in arms.)
I talk to baby quietly.
(Look down.)
I look at him and smile.
(Smile.)
I really like to sit and hold,
The baby for awhile.

Books to Share

French, Simon and Donna Rawlins. *Guess the Baby.* Houghton Mifflin, 2002. When Sam takes his baby brother to school, the other students and their teacher are delighted.

Leuck, Laura. *Goodnight, Baby Monster.* HarperCollins, 2002. A bedtime story for spooky things everywhere.

Meyers, Susan. *Everywhere Babies.* Harcourt, 2001. Explains that every day, everywhere, babies are carried, kissed, cared for and loved.

Newman, Marjorie. *Mole and the Baby Bird.* Bloomsbury, 2002. Mole finds a baby bird that has fallen from its nest. He takes care of it and wants to keep it, but ultimately learns that when you love something, you should let it be free.

Radunsky, Vladimir. *Ten: A Wonderful Story.* Viking, 2002. Mr. and Mrs. Armadillo, a very happy couple, are delighted that they are expecting a baby. Not one but ten babies arrive, and the relatives bring a variety of gifts.

Doorknob Hanger

Directions
Copy the pattern for each child and cut out. At story-time, have the children color it. Explain that they can hang this on the door when baby is sleeping to remind everyone in the house to play quietly.

 This craft takes 10 minutes to complete if all parts are precut.

One Potato Two Potato

In honor of National Potato Month during September.

Before Sharing Books

Bring several potatoes of different sizes and colors. Ask the children to tell you which is the smallest, largest, lumpiest and smoothest. Ask them to tell you some of their favorite ways to eat potatoes.

Rest Activities

Songs

"I Am a French Fry"
(Sung to the tune: "I'm a Little Teapot")
I am a French fry,
Tall and thin.
Open your mouth
And put me in.
I taste good with ketchup,
Sure enough.
So dip me in it
And chew me up.

"Mashed Potatoes"
(Sung to the tune: "Ten Little Indians")
Mounds and mounds of mashed potatoes,
Mounds and mounds of mashed potatoes,
Mounds and mounds of mashed potatoes,
I like them with butter.
Repeat with gravy, ketchup and peas.

Game

One Potato Two Potato

(Adapted Traditional Game)
Have the children stand in a circle and hold out a fist. Stand inside the circle. Tap your fist on the children's fists one by one while saying:

"One potato, two potato, three potato, four. Five potato, six potato, seven potato more."

The last child tapped puts his hand down. Repeat a few times.

Books to Share

Davis, Aubrey. *The Enormous Potato.* Kids Can Press, 1998. A farmer plants a potato that grows to be the biggest potato in the world. He requires the help of his wife, daughter, dog, cat and mouse to pull it out.

Jackson, Ellen. *The Impossible Riddle.* Charlesbridge Publishing, 1995. A czar of Russia loves his daughter—and her potato pancakes—so much that he doesn't want her to marry and leave him.

Rockwell, Anne. *Sweet Potato Pie.* Random House, 1996. Rhyming story follows the joyful gathering of a family around the table where Grandma has presented her baked sweet potato pie specialty.

Shiefman, Vicky. *Sunday Potatoes, Monday Potatoes.* Simon & Schuster, 1994. A family is poor and has nothing to eat but potatoes—every night. The best meal is on Saturday, when they have a fancy potato pudding (recipe included).

Potato Prints

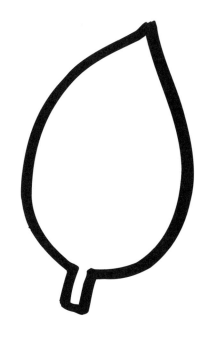

Directions

Protect the tables with newspapers. Provide protective aprons or shirts to keep paint off the children's clothing. Cut two large potatoes in half. Copy the patterns and cut out on potato halves to make stamps. At storytime, give the children white construction paper. Set out shallow dishes of tempera paint in a variety of colors. Let the children dip the potato in the paint, then press it on the construction paper. They may want to repeat the design several times or try one of the other shapes.

 This craft takes 10 minutes to complete if the potato stamps are premade.

Let's Do Lunch!

In honor of Eat Better, Eat Together Month during October.

Before Sharing Books

Bring in several lunch containers. You may choose to bring a picnic basket, a child's lunch box or a bag from one or two fast food restaurants, for example. Ask the children to think of something that might be inside each container such as an apple, a container of milk, a bag of chips or a piece of chicken. Let them talk about their favorite foods for lunch. Then open up the picnic basket, take out a book and begin your stories.

Rest Activities

Song

"Making a Sandwich"
(Sung to the tune: "Baby Bumblebee")
I'm going to make a sandwich, wait and see.
You will be so very proud of me.
The bread goes on the bottom, so yummy!
It's almost a sandwich!

I'm going to make a sandwich, wait and see.
You will be so very proud of me.
The cheese goes in the middle, so yummy!
It's almost a sandwich!

I'm going to make a sandwich, wait and see.
You will be so very proud of me.
The lettuce goes in the middle, so yummy!
It's almost a sandwich!

Add more verses here if you wish: tomatoes, pickles, ham, mustard.

I'm going to make a sandwich, wait and see.
You will be so very proud of me.
The bread goes on the top. So yummy!
NOW it is a sandwich!

Action Rhymes

Sharing Fruit
An apple tastes best when you share.
(Rub tummy and lick lips.)
Sharing is caring, so care to share.
(Hold out hands, palm up.)
A slice for me. A slice for you. So there.
(Pretend to slice fruit with finger.)
An apple tastes best when you share.
(Rub tummy and lick lips.)
Repeat using orange, banana, kiwi, etc.

My Tummy Can Talk
My tummy tells me when it's almost time for lunch.
(Point to tummy.)
If you listen you may hear it, too.
(Hand by ear.)
My tummy growls like a hungry little bear.
(Make a scary face and growl.)
Does your tummy do that, too?
(Point to someone.)

Books to Share

Blos, Joan W. *The Hungry Little Boy*. Simon & Schuster, 1995. A grandmother prepares her grandson's favorite meal, and then goes outside to play with him.

Gershator, David. *Bread Is For Eating*. Henry Holt & Company, 1995. A mother explains in English and Spanish how wheat is planted, harvested, milled and baked into loaves of bread.

London, Jonathan. *Crunch Munch*. Harcourt, 2001. Explores the sounds animals make as they enjoy their food.

Rubel, Nicole. *No More Vegetables!* Farrar, Straus and Giroux, 2002. Nothing will convince Ruthie to eat vegetables. She sings, "Give me a yucky carrot. I'll feed it to the parrot." Finally her mother says she doesn't have to eat any more vegetables if she will help her mother work in the garden.

Lunch Bunch Medallions

Directions

Copy two lunch bunch medallions for each child and cut out. Punch a hole in each medallion where indicated with a paper punch. Cut two pieces of yarn or string 30" in length for each child. At storytime, have the children color the medallions. Insert string and tie the ends. The child may give one medallion away to a parent, friend or sibling and wear the other one him or herself. Then the two of them can enjoy lunch together as the "lunch bunch."

 This craft takes 10 minutes to complete if all parts are precut.

Let's Go!

In honor of International Frugal Fun Day, the first Saturday in October. This is a day to explore free and low-cost activities such as going on a hike, picnic or car trip.

Before Sharing Books

Take the children on a pretend walk in the park. Do you hear someone bouncing a basketball? Can you see someone walking a dog? Do you smell hot dogs at the hot dog stand? Do you hear ducks quacking on the lake? Can you see a child coming down the slide? Can you hear a baby laughing in her stroller? Can you hear the old man snoring? Do you see the pretty kite in the air?

Rest Activities

Song

"Fun Activities"
(Sung to the tune: "Row, Row, Row Your Boat")
Ride, ride, ride your trike,
Up and down the street.
Peddling, peddling, peddling, peddling,
Fun that can't be beat.

Bounce, bounce, bounce your ball,
Up and down the street.
Bounce it, chase it, bounce it, chase it,
Fun that can't be beat.

Action Rhyme

I Have Two Feet
I have two feet for walking,
(Walk in place.)
I do it every day.
I have two feet for jumping,
(Jump in place.)
It's a fun way to play.

I have two feet for dancing,
(Dance in a circle.)
I like to dance this way.
I have two feet for standing,
(Stand still.)
I use my feet each day.

Fingerplay

Fly Around the World
This little duck and this little bird,
(Hold up two hands.)
Wanted to travel and see the world.
(Hold hand above eyebrows and look around.)
The bird said, "Cheep," and the duck said, "Quack."
(Make each hand talk.)
And they flew around the world and back.
(Hands make a big circle in the air.)

Books to Share

Gorbachev, Valeri. *Nicky and the Rainy Day*. North-South Books, 2002. On a rainy day, Nicky comes up with some imaginary journeys to pass the time until the rain clears.

Hendry, Diana. *The Very Busy Day*. Dutton, 2002. Big mouse grumbles as he works in the garden while little mouse daydreams. But big mouse is pleasantly surprised when he sees that little mouse has prepared a picnic.

Hort, Lenny. *The Seals on the Bus*. Henry Holt & Company, 2000. Seals, geese, rabbits, monkeys and more noisy critters join a family on a bus ride to the fair.

Hutchins, Pat. *We're Going on a Picnic*. HarperCollins, 2002. Hen, Duck and Goose set off to find the perfect spot for a picnic. They do not see a critter climb into their picnic basket to help itself to the berries, apples and pears inside.

Picnic Basket

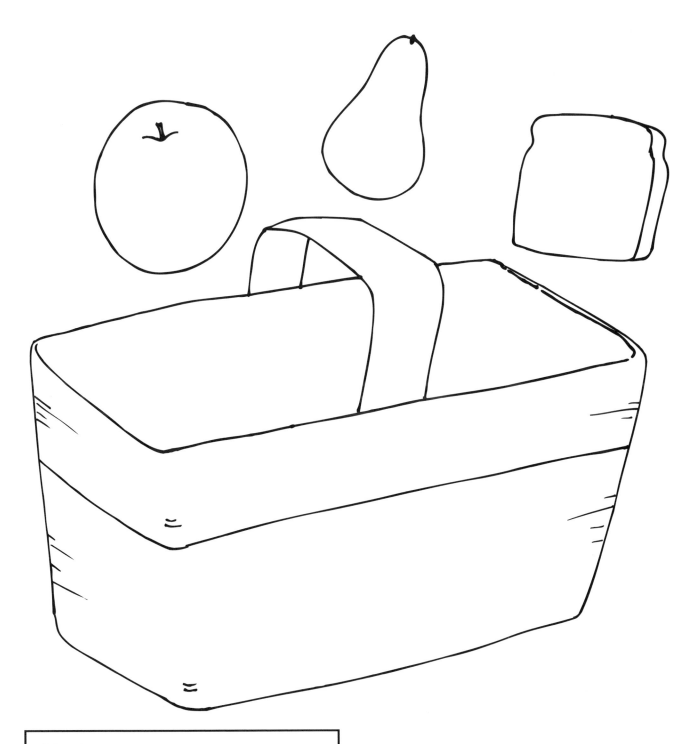

Directions
Copy the picnic basket and food patterns for each child and cut out. At storytime, have the children glue the fruit in the basket using a glue stick. They may color the fruit with crayons if desired.

This craft takes **10 minutes to complete if all parts are precut.**

Read to Me

In honor of National Family Literacy Day, November 1.

Before Sharing Books

Set out a variety of materials for reading: magazines, newspapers, cereal boxes, maps, telephone books, menus, video boxes and storybooks. Talk about your early memories of reading together with parents or other family members. Explain to the children that because you enjoyed hearing someone read to you as a child, you wanted to learn how to read for yourself, and now you can read anything you like. Tell the children how much you enjoy reading good books to them!

Rest Activities

Songs

"Read to Me"
(Sung to the tune: "Mary Had a Little Lamb")
Every day please read to me,
Read to me, read to me.
Every day please read to me.
I love to hear you read.

"Read a Book"
(Sung to the tune: "If You're Happy And You Know It")
If you like a happy story,
Read a book.
If you like a happy story,
Read a book.
If you like a happy story,
Then you'll never have to worry,
You can have a happy story!
Read a book.
Repeat with: scary story, true story, adventure story.

Fingerplay

Family Fun
My family is fun.
(Hold up five fingers.)
My mother likes to sing.
(Touch index finger.)
My father likes to hike.
(Touch middle finger.)
My sister likes to dance.
(Touch ring finger.)
My brother rides a bike.
(Touch little finger.)
I like to play
(Touch thumb.)
And go to the zoo.
At the end of the day,
Guess what we do?
We gather together,
To read a book or two!
(Curl fingers to make a fist.)

Books to Share

Hill, Susan. *Stuart at the Library.* HarperCollins, 2001. Stuart Little plans a peaceful afternoon at the library, but Bookworm, the library's owl, plans to make a meal of him.

Hopkins, Lee Bennett. *Climb Into My Lap: Poems to Read Together.* Simon & Schuster, 1998. This collection includes story poems, fingerplays, familiar verses and newly commissioned poems. Nicely illustrated.

Nakamura, Katherine Riley. *Song of Night: It's Time to Go to Bed.* Blue Sky Press, 2002. Eight parent/child animal pairs get ready for bed by singing lullabies and reading books.

Pak, Soyung. *Dear Juno.* Viking, 1999. A Korean-American boy, Juno, receives a letter. He knows by the stamp and the envelope that it is from his Korean grandmother. His parents must read the letter to him since it is in Korean, but she includes items he can "read," a photograph and pressed flowers.

Book of Rhymes

Trot, trot to Boston,
To buy a fat pig.
Home again.
Home again.
Jiggety jig.

Jack and Jill,
Went up the hill,
To fetch a pail of water.
Jack fell down,
And broke his crown,
And Jill came tumbling after.

Jack, be nimble.
Jack, be quick.
Jack, jump over,
The candlestick.

Here is the beehive.
Where are the bees?
Hidden away,
Where nobody sees.
Soon you will see them,
Come out of the hive.
1, 2, 3, 4, 5.

Directions
Copy the book pages for each child. Cut on the solid line. Fold on the dotted line. Make a cover for each book from construction paper, 5½" x 8½". Fold the cover. Assemble the book. Staple on dotted line. At storytime, read the rhymes aloud. Have the children draw an illustration for each rhyme with crayons.

 This craft takes 10 minutes to complete if all parts are precut and assembled.

Warm as Toast!

In honor of the Great American Warm-Up, a day to clean out closets and donate warm jackets, scarves, hats and mittens to charities. Annually, the second full week in November.

Before Sharing Books

Bring some child-size warm clothing, such as hats, scarves, mittens, etc. Ask, "What should you wear to keep your head warm?" The child who answers can come to the front and wear the hat. Continue until all items of clothing that you brought have been discussed.

Optional: Make arrangements with a charity that provides warm clothing for the needy. Have a warm clothing donation box available at storytime. Be sure to tell families a week or two ahead that you will be collecting warm clothing for charity at this storytime.

Rest Activities

Songs

"The Turtle Wears a Shell"
(Sung to the tune: "A Hunting We Will Go")
The turtle wears a shell.
The turtle wears a shell.
That is why he's warm and dry.
The turtle wears a shell.

"Dress for Chilly Weather"
(Sung to the tune: "Early in the Morning")
This is the way to zip your coat,
Zip your coat, zip your coat.
This is the way to zip your coat,
To dress for chilly weather.

This is the way to wrap your scarf,
Wrap your scarf, wrap your scarf.
This is the way to wrap your scarf,
To dress for chilly weather.

This is the way to tie your shoes,
Tie your shoes, tie your shoes.
This is the way to tie your shoes,
To dress for chilly weather.

Action Rhyme

Warm as Toast
I like my hat, *(Place hands on head.)*
My gloves, *(Clap hands.)*
My coat. (*Cross arms over body.)*
They keep me warm as toast.
At night when I climb into bed,
(Pretend to pull blanket to chin.)
I like my blanket most.
The wind may blow, *(Wave hands over head.)*
The rain may fall, *(Wiggle fingers in the air.)*
But I'm not cold,
No, not at all. *(Shake head.)*
I am as warm as I can be.
Warm! Warm as toast.
(Cross arms over body and smile.)

Books to Share

Birchall, Mark. *Rabbit's Wooly Sweater.* Lerner Publishing Group, 2001. Aunty Ethel knits Rabbit a new sweater, but Rabbit wants one for her toy blue bunny, Mr. Cuddles, too.

Lacome, Julie. *Ruthie's Big Old Coat.* Candlewick Press, 2000. Ruthie and her friend Fiona dance and play in a big old red hand-me-down coat.

Stoeke, Janet Morgan. *A Hat for Minerva Louise.* Penguin, 1994. A hen ventures out of the henhouse on a cold morning, and finds just the right thing to wear to keep her warm.

Wolff, Ferida. *The Woodcutter's Coat.* Little, Brown and Company. 1992. A thief steals the woodcutter's fine new coat, starting it on a merry journey through the village and finally back to the woodcutter.

Mitten Match Up

Directions
Copy the coloring sheet for each child. Instruct the children to draw a line to connect the mittens that match. Have the children color the mittens.

 This craft takes 5 minutes to complete.

Penguin Parade

In honor of the anniversary of the discovery of the South Pole, December 14, 1911.

Before Sharing Books

Teach the children how to walk like a penguin. Stand up tall. Put your feet close together. With arms at your sides, extend your hands slightly for wings. Now take tiny steps and waddle in place. When everyone is penguin perfect, parade around the storytime area. When children are back to their places, tell them to find a place to sit on the iceberg for some penguin stories.

Rest Activities

Song

"Penguin Walk"
(Sung to the tune: "Did You Ever See a Lassie?")
Did you ever see a penguin,
A penguin, a penguin.
Did you ever see a penguin,
Walk this way and that?
Walk this way and that way,
Walk this way and that way,
Did you ever see a penguin,
Walk this way and that?

Action Rhymes

Penguin Parade
Five little penguins, *(Hold up five fingers.)*
Black and white,
Got all dressed up,
On a Saturday night.
One wore a top hat. *(Touch head.)*
One held a cane.
(Hold out fist as if holding a cane.)
One wore a spotted tie. *(Hands at neck.)*
One's tie was plain.
One brushed his coat, *(Brush left arm, then right arm.)*
Until it was shiny.
Then they all went out,
Big, tall and tiny. *(Show sizes with hand.)*
Five little penguins *(Hold up five fingers.)*
Dressed up so fine,
Paraded down the street,
(Walk in place like a penguin.)
Until half past nine.

Penguin Splash
Wiggle your tail, *(Wiggle body.)*
Squat down low, *(Bend knees.)*
One, two, three,
Here we go! *(Jump.)*
SPLASH!!!

Books to Share

Lester, Helen. *Tackylocks and the Three Bears.* Houghton Mifflin, 2002. Tacky the penguin joins his friends Goodly, Lovely, Angel, Neatly and Perfect in putting on a play for Miss Beakley's class.

Murphy, Mary. *My Puffer Train.* Houghton Mifflin, 1999. Penguin sets off for the seashore in his puffer train, and along the way he invites a variety of animals to come on board.

Rey, Margret and H. A. *Whiteblack the Penguin Sees the World.* Houghton Mifflin, 2000. A penguin goes on a journey to find good stories for his radio show. He is shipwrecked on an iceberg, crosses the desert on a camel and falls out of an airplane. He returns home with plenty of new stories to share.

Wiesmuller, Dieter. *The Adventures of Marco and Polo.* Walker & Co., 2000. Marco Monkey and Polo Penguin meet by chance when a cruise ship puts in at the South Pole. Soon they are best friends. They visit each other's homelands, and try to find someplace where they can both live comfortably.

Penguin Dress Up

Directions
Copy the patterns for each child and cut out. Have the children dress the penguin by gluing on the top hat and tie with a glue stick. Have them color their penguins, if desired.

 This craft takes 5 minutes to complete if all parts are precut.

Texas Tales

In honor of the anniversary of the admission of the state of Texas, December 29, 1845.

Before Sharing Books

Dress yourself, or a puppet, in a cowboy hat, vest and bandanna scarf. Tell the children to pack their saddle bags, and get ready for a ride on the wide open plains of Texas. Ask, "What should you put in your saddle bags?" Suggest a canteen of water, a blanket, some trail mix and maybe a harmonica because cowboys and cowgirls like to have music by the campfire at night.

Rest Activities

Action Rhymes

I Am A Cowboy

I am a cowboy. *(Pretend to put cowboy hat on head.)*
See me ride, *(Pat lap to make sound of a horse.)*
With my dog running, *(Run in place.)*
By my side.
We take care,
Of the cattle all day,
(Hands on head to form the horns of a cow.)
And we rest by the campfire,
At the end of the day. *(Yawn and stretch.)*

Tumbleweeds

Out on the prairie,
The sun is hot. *(Arms form a circle over head.)*
The ground is hard and dry. *(Touch the ground.)*
But if a breeze begins, *(Wave arms.)*
You are sure to see, *(Hand on forehead, look around.)*
Tumbleweeds tumbling by.
(Circle one hand around the other.)

Fingerplays

Nighttime Prairie Sounds

One coyote howls to the moon.
(Hold up one finger.)
Two crickets chirp a tune.
(Hold up two fingers.)
Three owls call "Who" as they look around.
(Hold up three fingers.)
How I love the prairie sounds.

Texas Bluebonnets

Pretty stalks of blue and white,
(Hold up two fingers.)
In the green prairie grass.
The Texas flowers say hello,
(Wiggle fingers.)
To strangers as they pass.

Books to Share

Brett, Jan. *Armadillo Rodeo.* Putnam, 1995. A young armadillo named Bo wanders away from home and finds himself at the Curly H rodeo, where he rides a horse and kicks up his heels at a barn dance.

Cox, Judy. *The West Texas Chili Monster.* Troll Communications, 2003. The delicious smell from a chili cook-off attracts a space creature that eats all the chili in sight.

Harper, Jo. *Jalapeno Hal.* Eakin Press, 1997. Jalapeno Hal is the toughest hombre in Texas. He also has the meanest breath because he loves to eat hot peppers.

He has an unusual remedy for a drought that hits the town of Presidio.

Nixon, Joan Lowery. *That's the Spirit, Claude.* Penguin, 1994. Bessie and her brother Tom are hoping Sandy Clause comes to Texas at Christmastime.

Rubel, Nicole. *A Cowboy Named Earnestine.* Dial, 2001. When Earnestine O'Reilly arrives from Ireland as a mail-order bride, her husband-to-be is not what she expected. So she dons a Stetson hat and cowboy boots and joins a group of cattle herders where she finds true love at last.

Texas Bluebonnet Picture

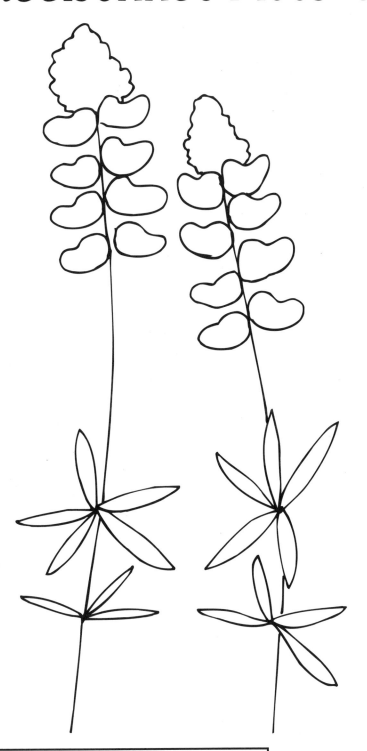

Directions

Enlarge and copy the pattern for each child. Cut about twenty 2" squares of blue and white tissue paper for each child. At storytime, have the children scrunch the tissue paper squares and glue them on the bluebonnet blossoms. They may color the stalk and leaves green, if desired.

 This craft takes 10 minute to complete if all parts are precut.

Theme Bibliography

January

Clean and Neat

(In honor of Organize Your Home Day.)

Count Down to Clean Up by Nancy Elizabeth Wallace. Houghton Mifflin, 2001.

Everything Has a Place by Patricia Lillie. Greenwillow Books, 1993.

Maisy Cleans Up by Lucy Cousins. Candlewick Press, 2002.

The Saturday Escape by Daniel J. Mahoney. Houghton Mifflin, 2002.

My Favorite Things

(In honor of Hunt for Happiness Week.)

Auntee Edna by Ethel Footman Smothers. William B. Eerdmans Publishing Company, 2001.

Even Firefighters Hug their Moms by Christine Kole MacLean. Dutton, 2002.

A Fine, Fine School by Sharon Creech. HarperCollins, 2001.

Greetings, Sun by Phillis and David Gershator. DK Publishing, 1998.

In My New Yellow Shirt by Eileen Spinelli. Henry Holt & Company, 2001.

February

I Like to Share

(In honor of Lost Penny Day, February 12, Abraham Lincoln's Birthday.)

Five Little Fiends by Sarah Dyer. Bloomsbury, 2002.

How Hungry Are You? by Donna Jo Napoli and Richard Tchen. Simon & Schuster, 2001.

Jubal's Wish by Audrey Wood. Blue Sky Press, 2000.

Ling Cho and His Three Friends by V. J. Pacilio. Farrar, Straus and Giroux, 2000.

Traveling Cows

(In honor of the anniversary of the first cow to be milked while flying in an airplane, February 18, 1930.)

Cappuccina Goes to Town by Mary Ann Smith. Kids Can Press, 2002.

The Cow Who Wouldn't Come Down by Paul Brett Johnson. Orchard Books, 1993.

Mrs. Mooley by Jack Kent. Golden Books, 2002.

Sailor Moo: Cow at Sea by Lisa Wheeler. Simon & Schuster, 2002.

March

Pigs Are Smart

(In honor of National Pig Day, March 1.)

A Cake All for Me! by Karen Magnuson Beil. Holiday House, 1998.

The Good Little Bad Little Pig by Margaret Wise Brown. Hyperion, 2002.

Those Can-Do Pigs by David McPhail. Penguin, 1996.

Toot and Puddle: Top of the World by Holly Hobbie. Little, Brown and Company, 2002.

It's Raining, It's Pouring

(In honor of National Umbrella Month.)

Gullywasher Gulch by Marianne Mitchell. Boyds Mills Press, 2004.

One Rainy Day by Valeri Gorbachev. Philomel, 2001.

The Rain Came Down by David Shannon. Scholastic, 2000.

Rain Romp by Jane Kurtz. HarperCollins, 2002.

Tessa's Tip-tapping Toes by Carolyn Crimi. Orchard Books, 2002.

April

Tickle My Funny Bone

(In honor of National Humor Month.)

Harry, I Need You! by Seymour Chwast. Houghton Mifflin, 2002.

Edwurd Fudwupper Fibbed Big by Berkeley Breathed. Little, Brown and Company, 2000.

Silly Sally by Audrey Wood. Harcourt, 1992.

Toestomper and the Caterpillars by Sharleen Collicott. Houghton Mifflin, 1999.

Sibling Silliness

(In honor of National Sibling Day, April 10.)

Bunbun, the Middle One by Sharon Pierce McCullough. Barefoot Books, 2001.

The Chicken Sisters by Laura Numeroff. HarperCollins, 1999.

Darcy and Gran Don't Like Babies by Jane Cutler. Farrar, Straus and Giroux, 2002.

Goldie Locks Has Chicken Pox by Erin Dealey. Simon & Schuster, 2002.

Stella, Fairy of the Forest by Marie-Louise Gay. Groundwood Books, 2002.

May

Rhyme Time

(In honor of Mother Goose Day, May 1.)

Hickory, Dickory, Dock by Robin Muller. Scholastic, 1994.

Humpty Dumpty by Daniel Kirk. Putnam, 2002.

Over the Candlestick: Classic Nursery Rhymes and the Real Stories Behind Them by Michael Montgomery. Peachtree Publishers, 2002.

Teddy Bear's Mother Goose by Michael Hague. Henry Holt & Company, 2001.

Going Visiting

(In honor of Visit Your Relatives Day, May 18.)

Great Aunt Martha by Rebecca C. Jones. Penguin, 1995.

Guess Who's Coming, Jesse Bear? by Nancy White Carlstrom. Simon & Schuster, 2002.

I Love Saturdays y Domingos by Alma Flor Ada. Simon & Schuster, 2001.

Sunday by Synthia St. James. Albert Whitman, 1996.

June

Talented Dogs

(In honor of Take Your Dog to Work Day.)

Dashing Dog! by Margaret Mahy. HarperCollins, 2002.

Dog Food by Saxton Freymann and Joost Elffers. Scholastic, 2002.

Dogs, Dogs, Dogs by Leslea Newman. Simon & Schuster, 2002.

Muldoon by Pamela Duncan Edwards. Hyperion, 2002.

Ten Silly Dogs: A Countdown Story by Lisa Flather. Orchard Books, 1999.

Happy Birthday

(In honor of the anniversary of the song "Happy Birthday to You.")

Elephant Pie by Hilda Offen. Penguin, 1993.

Happy Birthday, Lulu! by Caroline Uff. Walker & Co., 2000.

It's My Birthday, Too! by Lynne Jonell. Penguin, 2001.

Tiny Rabbit Goes to a Birthday Party by John Wallace. Holiday House, 2000.

What's Alice Up To? by Harley Jessup. Viking, 1997.

July

The Moon and Other Wonders

(In honor of the anniversary of man's first landing on the moon, July 20, 1969.)

The Moon Ring by Randy DuBurke. Chronicle Books, 2002.

Papa, Please Get the Moon for Me by Eric Carle. Simon & Schuster, 1991.

The Sea of Tranquility by Mark Haddon. HarperCollins, 1996.

Zoom! Zoom! Zoom! I'm Off to the Moon! by Dan Yaccarino. Scholastic, 1997.

Be Kind to Carrots

(In honor of National Salad Week.)

A is for Salad by Mike Lester. Putnam, 2002.

Cecil's Garden by Holly Keller. HarperCollins, 2002.

Old MacDonald Had an Apartment House by Judi Barrett. Simon & Schuster, 1998.

The Surprise Garden by Zoe Hall. Scholastic, 1998.

August

Bear Rally

(In honor of Amherst's Teddy Bear Rally.)

Bear Day by Cynthia Rylant. Harcourt, 1998.

The Bear on the Bed by Ruth Miller. Kids Can Press, 2002.

Big Bear Ball by Joanne Ryder. HarperCollins, 2002.

Oliver Finds His Way by Phyllis Root. Candlewick Press, 2002.

Traveling by Train

(In honor of the completion of the Transcontinental U.S. Railway, August 15, 1870.)

Dinosaur Train by John Steven Gurney. HarperCollins, 2002.

Two Little Trains by Margaret Wise Brown. HarperCollins, 2001.

Window Music by Anastasia Suen. Penguin Putnam, 1998.

September

Take Good Care of Your Baby

(In honor of Baby Safety Month.)

Everywhere Babies by Susan Meyers. Harcourt, 2001.

Goodnight, Baby Monster by Laura Leuck. HarperCollins, 2002.

Guess the Baby by Simon French and Donna Rawlins. Houghton Mifflin, 2002.

Mole and the Baby Bird by Marjorie Newman. Bloomsbury, 2002.

Ten: A Wonderful Story by Vladimir Radunsky. Viking, 2002.

One Potato Two Potato

(In honor of National Potato Month.)

The Enormous Potato by Aubrey Davis. Kids Can Press, 1998.

The Impossible Riddle by Ellen Jackson. Charlesbridge Publishing, 1995.

Sunday Potatoes, Monday Potatoes by Vicky Shiefman. Simon & Schuster, 1994.

Sweet Potato Pie by Anne Rockwell. Random House, 1996.

October

Let's Do Lunch!

(In honor of Eat Better, Eat Together Month.)

Bread is for Eating by David Gershator. Henry Holt & Company, 1995.

Crunch Munch by Jonathan London. Harcourt, 2001.

The Hungry Little Boy by Joan W. Blos. Simon & Schuster, 1995.

No More Vegetables! by Nicole Rubel. Farrar, Straus and Giroux, 2002.

Let's Go!

(In honor of International Frugal Fun Day.)

Nicky and the Rainy Day by Valeri Gorbachev. North-South Books, 2002.

The Seals on the Bus by Lenny Hort. Henry Holt & Company, 2000.

The Very Busy Day by Diana Hendry. Dutton, 2002.

We're Going on a Picnic by Pat Hutchins. HarperCollins, 2002.

November

Read to Me

(In honor of National Family Literacy Day, November 1.)

Climb Into My Lap: First Poems to Read Together by Lee Bennett Hopkins. Simon & Schuster, 1998.

Dear Juno by Soyung Pak. Viking, 1999.

Song of Night: It's Time to Go to Bed by Katherine Riley Nakamura. Blue Sky Press, 2002.

Stuart at the Library by Susan Hill. HarperCollins, 2001.

Warm as Toast!

(In honor of the Great American Warm-Up.)

A Hat for Minerva Louise by Janet Morgan Stoeke. Penguin, 1994.

Rabbit's Wooly Sweater by Mark Birchall. Lerner Publishing Group, 2001.

Ruthie's Big Old Coat by Julie Lacome. Candlewick Press, 2000.

The Woodcutter's Coat by Ferida Wolff. Little, Brown and Company, 1992.

December

Penguin Parade

(In honor of the anniversary of the discovery of the South Pole, December 14, 1911.)

The Adventures of Marco and Polo by Dieter Wiesmuller. Walker & Co., 2000.

My Puffer Train by Mary Murphy. Houghton Mifflin, 1999.

Tackylocks and the Three Bears by Helen Lester. Houghton Mifflin, 2002.

Whiteblack the Penguin Sees the World by Margret and H. A. Rey. Houghton Mifflin, 2000.

Texas Tales

(In honor of the anniversary of the admission of the state of Texas, December 29, 1845.)

Armadillo Rodeo by Jan Brett. Putnam, 1995.

A Cowboy Named Earnestine by Nicole Rubel. Dial, 2001.

Jalapeno Hal by Jo Harper. Eakin Press, 1997.

That's the Spirit, Claude by Joan Lowery Nixon. Penguin, 1994.

The West Texas Chili Monster by Judy Cox. Troll Communications, 2003.